"Big Data Science"

Basic Concepts and Applications

Table of Content:

Article

1. Introduction to Data Science

Introduction

Data Science is a rapidly evolving field that has become integral to numerous industries. Understanding its core aspects can provide a solid foundation for anyone looking to dive into this exciting domain. In this section, we will explore three main sub-points:

1. **What is Data Science?**
2. **The Importance of Data Science**
3. **The Evolution of Data Science**

1. What Is Data Science?

Data Science is a multidisciplinary field that uses scientific methods, processes, algorithms, and systems to extract knowledge and insights from structured and unstructured data. It encompasses techniques and theories from fields like mathematics, statistics, computer science, and information technology. Here, we'll delve deeper into what makes up this fascinating field.

1.1 The Core Components of Data Science

At its heart, Data Science is composed of several key components:

- **Statistics and Mathematics**: These form the backbone of data science. Statistical methods help in understanding and analyzing data patterns, while mathematics provides the theoretical framework for developing algorithms.

- **Computer Science**: Programming is essential in data science for handling data, implementing algorithms, and building models. Languages like Python and R are particularly popular among data scientists.
- **Domain Expertise**: Understanding the specific industry or field where data science is applied is crucial. Domain expertise allows data scientists to ask the right questions and interpret data in a meaningful context.
- **Data Engineering**: This involves the extraction, transformation, and loading (ETL) of data. Data engineers ensure that data is collected from various sources and prepared for analysis.
- **Machine Learning**: This subset of artificial intelligence involves creating algorithms that can learn from and make predictions or decisions based on data. Machine learning is a critical part of many data science projects.

1.2 The Data Science Process

The data science process typically involves several steps:

- **Data Collection**: Gathering data from various sources such as databases, web scraping, sensors, and more. This step is fundamental, as the quality of data collected will directly impact the results of the analysis.

- **Data Cleaning**: Raw data often contains noise, errors, or missing values. Data cleaning involves preprocessing the data to make it suitable for analysis. This step can be time-consuming but is essential for accurate results.
- **Data Exploration and Visualization**: Before diving into complex analyses, data scientists explore the data to understand its characteristics. Visualization tools like matplotlib, seaborn, and Tableau are used to create graphs and charts that reveal patterns and insights.
- **Model Building**: Using statistical and machine learning techniques, data scientists build models that can predict outcomes or classify data. This step involves selecting the appropriate algorithms and tuning their parameters for optimal performance.
- **Model Evaluation**: Once a model is built, it needs to be evaluated to ensure it performs well on unseen data. Techniques like cross-validation and metrics such as accuracy, precision, and recall are used to assess model performance.
- **Deployment and Monitoring**: The final step is deploying the model into a production environment where it can provide value. Continuous monitoring is necessary to ensure the model remains effective and to update it as needed.

1.3 Real-World Applications of Data Science

Data Science is not just a theoretical concept; it has numerous practical applications across various industries:

- **Healthcare**: Data science is used to predict disease outbreaks, personalize treatment plans, and improve patient outcomes. For instance, machine learning models can analyze medical images to detect diseases like cancer at an early stage.
- **Finance**: Financial institutions use data science for fraud detection, risk management, and algorithmic trading. Predictive models help banks assess credit risk and make informed lending decisions.
- **Marketing**: Companies leverage data science to understand customer behavior, segment their audience, and optimize marketing campaigns. Recommendation systems, like those used by Netflix and Amazon, are a classic example of data science in marketing.
- **E-commerce**: Online retailers use data science to manage inventory, predict sales trends, and enhance customer experiences through personalized recommendations.
- **Transportation**: From optimizing routes to developing autonomous vehicles, data science plays a crucial role in making transportation systems more efficient and safer.

2. The Importance of Data Science

Data Science has become increasingly important in today's data-driven world. Its significance can be understood through its impact on decision-making, innovation, and operational efficiency.

2.1 Data-Driven Decision Making

In the past, decisions in business and other fields were often based on intuition and experience. Today, data science provides a more empirical basis for decision-making. By analyzing large datasets, organizations can uncover insights that would be impossible to detect manually. This leads to more informed and objective decisions.

- **Predictive Analytics**: Businesses use predictive models to forecast future trends and behaviors. For instance, retailers can predict which products will be popular in the next season, allowing them to manage inventory more effectively.
- **Descriptive Analytics**: This involves analyzing historical data to understand what has happened in the past. It helps organizations learn from past experiences and make improvements.
- **Prescriptive Analytics**: Going a step further, prescriptive analytics suggests actions based on the data. It answers the question, "What should we do?" For example, an airline might use prescriptive analytics to set optimal pricing for tickets based on various factors like demand, season, and competition.

2.2 Driving Innovation

Data Science fuels innovation by providing new insights and enabling the development of new products and services. It helps companies stay competitive in a rapidly changing market.

- **Product Development**: By analyzing customer feedback and usage patterns, companies can design products that better meet the needs of their customers. Data science can also identify opportunities for new product features or entirely new products.

- **Process Optimization**: Data science helps organizations optimize their processes, reducing waste and improving efficiency. For instance, manufacturers can use predictive maintenance to anticipate equipment failures and prevent costly downtime.

- **Enhanced Customer Experience**: Understanding customer preferences and behavior allows companies to tailor their offerings and interactions, providing a more personalized experience. This can lead to increased customer satisfaction and loyalty.

2.3 Operational Efficiency

Data Science can significantly improve operational efficiency in various ways:

- **Automation**: Many routine tasks can be automated using data science techniques, freeing up human resources for more complex and creative tasks. For instance, chatbots powered by natural language processing can handle customer inquiries, reducing the workload on customer service teams.

- **Resource Management**: Data science helps in optimizing resource allocation, ensuring that the right resources are available at the right time. This is particularly important in industries like logistics and supply chain management.

- **Risk Management**: By analyzing data, organizations can identify potential risks and take proactive measures to mitigate them. This is crucial in industries such as finance, where risk management is a key component of operations.

3. The Evolution of Data Science

Data Science has come a long way from its early days. Understanding its evolution helps us appreciate its current state and anticipate future developments.

3.1 Early Beginnings

The roots of data science can be traced back to statistics and data analysis, which have been used for centuries. However, the term "data science" itself is relatively new, first appearing in the 1960s. Early data analysis was primarily done manually, with statisticians and analysts working with small datasets.

3.2 The Advent of Computers

The invention of computers revolutionized data science. In the 1950s and 60s, computers began to be used for data processing, allowing for the analysis of much larger datasets. This period saw the development of early databases and the first use of statistical software.

3.3 The Rise of Big Data

The term "big data" emerged in the early 2000s, describing the massive volumes of data generated by modern technologies such as the internet, social media, and IoT devices. Traditional data processing methods were no longer sufficient, leading to the development of new technologies and frameworks like Hadoop and Spark.

3.4 The Age of Machine Learning

Machine learning has become a core component of data science, enabling the creation of models that can learn from data and make predictions or decisions. The rise of machine learning has been driven by advances in algorithms, increased computing power, and the availability of large datasets.

3.5 The Current State of Data Science

Today, data science is a highly interdisciplinary field that combines elements of statistics, computer science, and domain expertise. It encompasses a wide range of techniques and tools, from simple data analysis to complex machine learning models.

3.6 The Future of Data Science

Looking ahead, data science is expected to continue evolving rapidly. Some trends to watch include:

- **Increased Automation**: Automation tools will make data science more accessible to non-experts, enabling a broader range of people to use data science techniques.
- **Real-Time Data Processing**: As the demand for real-time insights grows, data science will increasingly focus on real-time data processing and analysis.

- **Integration with AI**: The lines between data science and artificial intelligence will continue to blur, with more integrated AI solutions emerging.
- **Ethical Considerations**: As data science becomes more pervasive, ethical considerations around data privacy, bias, and fairness will become increasingly important.

In conclusion, data science is a dynamic and evolving field that plays a crucial role in modern society. Its applications are vast, and its impact is profound, driving innovation, improving decision-making, and enhancing operational efficiency. Whether you're a business leader, a tech enthusiast, or someone curious about the field, understanding data science is essential in today's data-driven world.

2. The Basics of Data Science
What is Data Science?
Data Science is a multidisciplinary field that combines statistics, computer science, and domain expertise to extract meaningful insights from data. It's all about transforming raw data into actionable knowledge.

Importance of Data Science
Data Science is crucial in today's data-driven world. It helps businesses make informed decisions, drives innovation, and improves operational efficiency.

3. Key Components of Data Science
Data Collection
Gathering data from various sources such as databases, online resources, sensors, and surveys is the first step in any data science project.

Data Cleaning

Raw data often contains errors, duplicates, or inconsistencies. Data cleaning involves preprocessing this data to ensure accuracy and reliability.

Data Analysis

This is where the magic happens. Data analysis involves applying statistical methods and algorithms to identify patterns, trends, and correlations.

Data Visualization

Presenting data in graphical formats like charts and graphs helps communicate findings effectively. Visualization makes complex data more accessible and understandable.

4. Tools and Technologies in Data Science

Programming Languages

Python and R are the go-to programming languages for data scientists due to their extensive libraries and ease of use.

Software and Platforms

Tools like Apache Hadoop, Spark, and cloud platforms like AWS and Google Cloud provide the infrastructure needed to handle large datasets.

Machine Learning Libraries

Libraries such as TensorFlow, Scikit-learn, and PyTorch are essential for building and deploying machine learning models.

5. Applications of Data Science

Healthcare

Data Science is revolutionizing healthcare with predictive analytics, personalized medicine, and improved diagnostic tools.

Finance

In finance, data science helps with fraud detection, risk management, algorithmic trading, and customer analytics.

Marketing

Marketers use data science to analyze consumer behavior, segment audiences, and optimize campaigns for better ROI.

E-commerce

Data science enhances customer experiences through recommendation systems, inventory management, and pricing strategies.

Transportation

From optimizing routes to developing autonomous vehicles, data science is key in making transportation more efficient.

6. The Role of a Data Scientist

Skills Required

A data scientist needs a blend of technical skills (like programming and machine learning) and soft skills (such as critical thinking and communication).

Daily Responsibilities

Data scientists spend their days collecting data, cleaning it, performing analysis, building models, and communicating results to stakeholders.

7. Data Science in the Future

Trends and Predictions

The future of data science includes advancements in AI, increased automation, and the integration of more real-time data processing.

8. Challenges in Data Science

Data Privacy Issues

Ensuring data privacy and security is a significant challenge, given the increasing amount of personal data being collected.

Handling Big Data

Managing and processing vast amounts of data requires robust infrastructure and sophisticated techniques.

9. Educational Pathways for Data Science

Academic Degrees

Many universities offer specialized degrees in data science, providing a solid foundation in the necessary skills and knowledge.

Online Courses and Bootcamps

For those looking to switch careers or upskill, online courses and bootcamps offer flexible and intensive training programs.

10. Conclusion

Data Science is an ever-evolving field that plays a critical role in various industries. It offers numerous career opportunities and helps drive innovation and efficiency. Whether you're looking to start a career in data science or just understand its impact, this field is worth exploring.

11. FAQs

What is the main purpose of data science?

The main purpose of data science is to analyze and interpret complex data to help make informed decisions and drive strategic initiatives.

What skills are essential for a data scientist?

Essential skills include programming, statistical analysis, machine learning, data visualization, and domain-specific knowledge.

How is data science used in everyday life?

Data science is used in various ways, from recommendation systems on streaming services to personalized advertising and smart home devices.

What are the challenges in becoming a data scientist?

Challenges include staying updated with the latest technologies, mastering diverse skills, and handling complex and large datasets.

Can I become a data scientist without a degree?

Yes, many have transitioned into data science through online courses, bootcamps, and self-study, though a formal education can provide a structured learning path.

Introduction to Data Science

Data Science is a rapidly evolving field that has become integral to numerous industries. Understanding its core aspects can provide a solid foundation for anyone looking to dive into this exciting domain. In this section, we will explore three main sub-points:

1. **What is Data Science?**
2. **The Importance of Data Science**
3. **The Evolution of Data Science**

1. What is Data Science?

Data Science is a multidisciplinary field that uses scientific methods, processes, algorithms, and systems to extract knowledge and insights from structured and unstructured data. It encompasses techniques and theories from fields like mathematics, statistics, computer science, and information technology. Here, we'll delve deeper into what makes up this fascinating field.

1.1 The Core Components of Data Science

At its heart, Data Science is composed of several key components:

- **Statistics and Mathematics**: These form the backbone of data science. Statistical methods help in understanding and analyzing data patterns, while mathematics provides the theoretical framework for developing algorithms.
- **Computer Science**: Programming is essential in data science for handling data, implementing algorithms, and building models. Languages like Python and R are particularly popular among data scientists.
- **Domain Expertise**: Understanding the specific industry or field where data science is applied is crucial. Domain expertise allows data scientists to ask the right questions and interpret data in a meaningful context.
- **Data Engineering**: This involves the extraction, transformation, and loading (ETL) of data. Data engineers ensure that data is collected from various sources and prepared for analysis.
- **Machine Learning**: This subset of artificial intelligence involves creating algorithms that can learn from and make predictions or decisions based on data. Machine learning is a critical part of many data science projects.

1.2 The Data Science Process

The data science process typically involves several steps:

- **Data Collection**: Gathering data from various sources such as databases, web scraping, sensors, and more. This step is fundamental, as the quality of data collected will directly impact the results of the analysis.
- **Data Cleaning**: Raw data often contains noise, errors, or missing values. Data cleaning involves preprocessing the data to make it suitable for analysis. This step can be time-consuming but is essential for accurate results.
- **Data Exploration and Visualization**: Before diving into complex analyses, data scientists explore the data to understand its characteristics. Visualization tools like matplotlib, seaborn, and Tableau are used to create graphs and charts that reveal patterns and insights.
- **Model Building**: Using statistical and machine learning techniques, data scientists build models that can predict outcomes or classify data. This step involves selecting the appropriate algorithms and tuning their parameters for optimal performance.
- **Model Evaluation**: Once a model is built, it needs to be evaluated to ensure it performs well on unseen data. Techniques like cross-validation and metrics such as accuracy, precision, and recall are used to assess model performance.
- **Deployment and Monitoring**: The final step is deploying the model into a production environment where it can provide value. Continuous monitoring is necessary to ensure the model remains effective and to update it as needed.

1.3 Real-World Applications of Data Science

Data Science is not just a theoretical concept; it has numerous practical applications across various industries:

- **Healthcare**: Data science is used to predict disease outbreaks, personalize treatment plans, and improve patient outcomes. For instance, machine learning models can analyze medical images to detect diseases like cancer at an early stage.
- **Finance**: Financial institutions use data science for fraud detection, risk management, and algorithmic trading. Predictive models help banks assess credit risk and make informed lending decisions.
- **Marketing**: Companies leverage data science to understand customer behavior, segment their audience, and optimize marketing campaigns. Recommendation systems, like those used by Netflix and Amazon, are a classic example of data science in marketing.
- **E-commerce**: Online retailers use data science to manage inventory, predict sales trends, and enhance customer experiences through personalized recommendations.
- **Transportation**: From optimizing routes to developing autonomous vehicles, data science plays a crucial role in making transportation systems more efficient and safer.

2. The Importance of Data Science

Data Science has become increasingly important in today's data-driven world. Its significance can be understood through its impact on decision-making, innovation, and operational efficiency.

2.1 Data-Driven Decision Making

In the past, decisions in business and other fields were often based on intuition and experience. Today, data science provides a more empirical basis for decision-making. By analyzing large datasets, organizations can uncover insights that would be impossible to detect manually. This leads to more informed and objective decisions.

- **Predictive Analytics**: Businesses use predictive models to forecast future trends and behaviors. For instance, retailers can predict which products will be popular in the next season, allowing them to manage inventory more effectively.
- **Descriptive Analytics**: This involves analyzing historical data to understand what has happened in the past. It helps organizations learn from past experiences and make improvements.
- **Prescriptive Analytics**: Going a step further, prescriptive analytics suggests actions based on the data. It answers the question, "What should we do?" For example, an airline might use prescriptive analytics to set optimal pricing for tickets based on various factors like demand, season, and competition.

2.2 Driving Innovation

Data Science fuels innovation by providing new insights and enabling the development of new products and services. It helps companies stay competitive in a rapidly changing market.

- **Product Development**: By analyzing customer feedback and usage patterns, companies can

design products that better meet the needs of their customers. Data science can also identify opportunities for new product features or entirely new products.
- **Process Optimization**: Data science helps organizations optimize their processes, reducing waste and improving efficiency. For instance, manufacturers can use predictive maintenance to anticipate equipment failures and prevent costly downtime.
- **Enhanced Customer Experience**: Understanding customer preferences and behavior allows companies to tailor their offerings and interactions, providing a more personalized experience. This can lead to increased customer satisfaction and loyalty.

2.3 Operational Efficiency

Data Science can significantly improve operational efficiency in various ways:

- **Automation**: Many routine tasks can be automated using data science techniques, freeing up human resources for more complex and creative tasks. For instance, chatbots powered by natural language processing can handle customer inquiries, reducing the workload on customer service teams.
- **Resource Management**: Data science helps in optimizing resource allocation, ensuring that the right resources are available at the right time. This is particularly important in industries like logistics and supply chain management.
- **Risk Management**: By analyzing data, organizations can identify potential risks and take

proactive measures to mitigate them. This is crucial in industries such as finance, where risk management is a key component of operations.

3. The Evolution of Data Science

Data Science has come a long way from its early days. Understanding its evolution helps us appreciate its current state and anticipate future developments.

3.1 Early Beginnings

The roots of data science can be traced back to statistics and data analysis, which have been used for centuries. However, the term "data science" itself is relatively new, first appearing in the 1960s. Early data analysis was primarily done manually, with statisticians and analysts working with small datasets.

3.2 The Advent of Computers

The invention of computers revolutionized data science. In the 1950s and 60s, computers began to be used for data processing, allowing for the analysis of much larger datasets. This period saw the development of early databases and the first use of statistical software.

3.3 The Rise of Big Data

The term "big data" emerged in the early 2000s, describing the massive volumes of data generated by modern technologies such as the internet, social media, and IoT devices. Traditional data processing methods were no longer sufficient, leading to the development of new technologies and frameworks like Hadoop and Spark.

3.4 The Age of Machine Learning

Machine learning has become a core component of data science, enabling the creation of models that can learn from data and make predictions or decisions. The rise of machine learning has been driven by advances in algorithms, increased computing power, and the availability of large datasets.

3.5 The Current State of Data Science

Today, data science is a highly interdisciplinary field that combines elements of statistics, computer science, and domain expertise. It encompasses a wide range of techniques and tools, from simple data analysis to complex machine learning models.

3.6 The Future of Data Science

Looking ahead, data science is expected to continue evolving rapidly. Some trends to watch include:

- **Increased Automation**: Automation tools will make data science more accessible to non-experts, enabling a broader range of people to use data science techniques.
- **Real-Time Data Processing**: As the demand for real-time insights grows, data science will increasingly focus on real-time data processing and analysis.
- **Integration with AI**: The lines between data science and artificial intelligence will continue to blur, with more integrated AI solutions emerging.
- **Ethical Considerations**: As data science becomes more pervasive, ethical considerations

around data privacy, bias, and fairness will become increasingly important.

In conclusion, data science is a dynamic and evolving field that plays a crucial role in modern society. Its applications are vast, and its impact is profound, driving innovation, improving decision-making, and enhancing operational efficiency. Whether you're a business leader, a tech enthusiast, or someone curious about the field, understanding data science is essential in today's data-driven world.

The Importance of Data Science

Data Science has emerged as a cornerstone of modern decision-making and innovation. Its importance spans across industries, influencing how businesses operate, compete, and evolve. This section will delve into the key aspects of why Data Science is essential in today's world by exploring three main sub-points:

1. **Data-Driven Decision Making**
2. **Driving Innovation**
3. **Operational Efficiency**

1. Data-Driven Decision Making

In an era where data is abundant and accessible, making informed decisions has become more achievable than ever. Data-Driven Decision Making (DDDM) leverages data to guide strategic and operational choices. Let's explore how Data Science enhances decision-making processes.

1.1 Predictive Analytics

Predictive analytics uses historical data to predict future outcomes. This aspect of data science is vital for businesses looking to anticipate trends and prepare for future scenarios. Here's how predictive analytics is applied:

- **Sales Forecasting**: Retailers use predictive models to forecast demand for products, helping them manage inventory and optimize supply chains. For example, during the holiday season, accurate predictions ensure that popular items are sufficiently stocked.
- **Customer Behavior**: By analyzing past customer interactions and transactions, companies can predict future behaviors such as purchase likelihood, customer churn, and lifetime value. This helps in tailoring marketing strategies to individual customer needs.
- **Risk Management**: Financial institutions apply predictive analytics to assess credit risk and detect potential fraud. For instance, by examining transaction patterns, banks can identify unusual activities that may indicate fraud.

1.2 Descriptive Analytics

Descriptive analytics focuses on summarizing historical data to understand what has happened in the past. This type of analysis is foundational for any data-driven strategy, providing insights that help businesses learn from previous experiences.

- **Performance Analysis**: Companies analyze past performance metrics to identify strengths and weaknesses. For example, a sales team might review quarterly sales data to understand which strategies worked and which did not.

- **Customer Insights**: By examining historical customer data, businesses can uncover trends and preferences. This information is crucial for developing products and services that better meet customer needs.
- **Operational Efficiency**: Descriptive analytics can highlight inefficiencies in business processes. For instance, analyzing production line data can reveal bottlenecks that need addressing.

1.3 Prescriptive Analytics

Prescriptive analytics goes beyond predicting future outcomes by suggesting actions to achieve desired results. It uses optimization and simulation algorithms to recommend the best course of action.

- **Supply Chain Optimization**: Companies use prescriptive analytics to manage their supply chains more effectively. For example, by simulating different scenarios, they can determine the optimal inventory levels to minimize costs and meet demand.
- **Resource Allocation**: Prescriptive models help businesses allocate resources efficiently. For example, a hospital might use these models to schedule staff shifts, ensuring optimal coverage while minimizing labor costs.
- **Marketing Strategies**: By combining customer data with prescriptive analytics, marketers can design targeted campaigns that maximize return on investment. For instance, they can determine the best mix of marketing channels and budget allocation.

1.4 Real-Time Decision Making

With the advent of real-time data processing technologies, businesses can make decisions on the fly. Real-time analytics enables immediate insights, which are crucial in fast-paced environments.

- **Stock Market Trading**: Real-time data is essential for algorithmic trading, where decisions must be made in fractions of a second to capitalize on market movements.
- **Customer Service**: Real-time analytics enhances customer support by providing agents with up-to-the-minute information about customer issues, leading to quicker and more effective resolutions.
- **Operations Management**: In industries like manufacturing, real-time data helps monitor equipment performance and detect anomalies, preventing downtime and maintaining smooth operations.

2. Driving Innovation

Data Science is a catalyst for innovation, enabling the development of new products, services, and business models. Let's explore how data science drives innovation across different domains.

2.1 Product Development

Data science plays a pivotal role in product development by providing insights that guide the creation of products that meet customer needs and preferences.

- **Market Analysis**: Companies use data science to analyze market trends and identify gaps in the market. This helps in developing products that are in demand. For instance, analyzing social media trends can reveal emerging consumer preferences.

- **Customer Feedback**: By analyzing customer reviews and feedback, businesses can identify areas for improvement in their products. This continuous feedback loop ensures that products evolve to meet customer expectations.
- **Prototype Testing**: Data science enables efficient testing of product prototypes. By analyzing data from prototype tests, companies can make data-driven decisions about which features to retain or modify.

2.2 Process Optimization

Optimizing business processes through data science leads to increased efficiency and cost savings. Here are some examples of how this is achieved:

- **Manufacturing**: Data science helps optimize manufacturing processes by analyzing production data. Predictive maintenance models can anticipate equipment failures, reducing downtime and maintenance costs.
- **Supply Chain Management**: Advanced analytics optimize supply chain operations by forecasting demand, managing inventory, and improving logistics. For instance, machine learning models can predict shipping delays and suggest alternative routes.
- **Energy Management**: Data science is used in the energy sector to optimize the use of resources. Smart grids analyze consumption

patterns and adjust energy distribution in real-time to improve efficiency and reduce costs.

2.3 Enhanced Customer Experience

Providing a personalized and seamless customer experience is crucial for retaining customers and gaining a competitive edge. Data science enables this through several methods:

- **Personalization**: Recommendation engines use data science to provide personalized suggestions to customers. For example, streaming services like Netflix recommend shows based on viewing history and preferences.
- **Customer Journey Analysis**: By analyzing customer interactions across different touchpoints, businesses can understand the customer journey and identify pain points. This helps in designing better customer experiences.
- **Chatbots and Virtual Assistants**: Natural language processing (NLP) and machine learning power chatbots and virtual assistants that provide personalized customer support, enhancing user satisfaction.

2.4 Competitive Advantage

Data science provides businesses with a competitive edge by enabling them to leverage data in strategic ways.

- **Market Positioning**: By analyzing competitors and market trends, companies can position themselves more effectively. For instance, analyzing pricing strategies of competitors helps in setting competitive prices.

- **Innovation in Services**: Data science enables the development of innovative services that differentiate a company from its competitors. For example, financial institutions offer personalized financial advice through AI-driven platforms.
- **Agility and Adaptability**: Companies that leverage data science can quickly adapt to changing market conditions. Real-time analytics allows for rapid response to new trends and opportunities.

2.5 Research and Development

Data science accelerates research and development (R&D) by providing insights that drive innovation and discovery.

- **Scientific Research**: In fields like genomics and pharmaceuticals, data science accelerates research by analyzing large datasets to identify patterns and correlations. This leads to faster drug discovery and development.
- **Technology Development**: Tech companies use data science to develop new technologies and improve existing ones. For instance, data-driven insights guide the development of more efficient algorithms and software.
- **Academic Research**: Universities and research institutions leverage data science for academic research across various disciplines. Analyzing large datasets from experiments and studies leads to new scientific discoveries.

3. Operational Efficiency

Operational efficiency is crucial for any organization aiming to reduce costs and improve productivity. Data Science enhances operational efficiency through several key applications.

3.1 Automation

Automation powered by data science reduces manual effort and increases efficiency in various business processes.

- **Robotic Process Automation (RPA)**: RPA uses bots to automate repetitive tasks such as data entry, invoice processing, and customer onboarding. This not only reduces errors but also frees up employees to focus on more strategic tasks.
- **Intelligent Automation**: Combining RPA with AI and machine learning creates intelligent automation systems capable of handling more complex tasks. For example, AI-driven chatbots can handle customer queries, providing instant support.
- **Workflow Optimization**: Data science helps in optimizing workflows by identifying bottlenecks and inefficiencies. For instance, analyzing employee performance data can reveal areas for process improvement.

3.2 Resource Management

Efficient resource management is essential for maximizing productivity and minimizing waste. Data science provides the tools needed to achieve this.

- **Human Resources**: Data science aids in workforce management by analyzing employee performance, predicting turnover, and optimizing recruitment processes. For instance, predictive models can identify employees at risk of leaving and suggest retention strategies.
- **Asset Management**: Companies use data science to monitor and manage physical assets. Predictive maintenance models help in scheduling maintenance activities proactively, extending the lifespan of equipment and reducing downtime.
- **Energy Efficiency**: Data science optimizes energy consumption in buildings and industrial processes. By analyzing usage patterns, companies can implement energy-saving measures and reduce costs.

3.3 Risk Management

Managing risk is critical for the stability and growth of any organization. Data science enhances risk management through predictive analytics and real-time monitoring.

- **Financial Risk**: Financial institutions use data science to assess credit risk, market risk, and operational risk. Predictive models help in identifying potential defaults and fraud, enabling proactive measures.
- **Operational Risk**: Data science helps in identifying and mitigating operational risks such as supply chain disruptions, equipment failures, and compliance issues. Real-time monitoring systems alert organizations to potential risks before they escalate.

- **Cybersecurity**: Data science plays a crucial role in cybersecurity by detecting anomalies and potential threats. Machine learning models analyze network traffic to identify suspicious activities, helping to prevent cyber-attacks.

3.4 Cost Reduction

Data science helps organizations reduce costs by optimizing processes and eliminating inefficiencies.

- **Supply Chain Optimization**: By analyzing supply chain data, companies can identify cost-saving opportunities in areas such as logistics, inventory management, and procurement.
- **Operational Efficiency**: Data science streamlines operations by automating tasks and optimizing workflows. This leads to significant cost savings by reducing manual labor and improving productivity.
- **Energy Savings**: Implementing data-driven energy management practices helps organizations reduce energy consumption and costs. For example, smart lighting systems adjust brightness based on occupancy and natural light levels.

3.5 Quality Control

Maintaining high-quality standards is essential for customer satisfaction and business success. Data science enhances quality control through advanced analytics and real-time monitoring.

- **Manufacturing Quality**: Data science helps in monitoring and controlling product quality in manufacturing processes. Machine learning models detect defects and anomalies, ensuring products meet quality standards.

- **Service Quality**: In service industries, data science analyzes customer feedback and service metrics to identify areas for improvement. This leads to enhanced service quality and customer satisfaction.
- **Compliance**: Ensuring compliance with regulations and standards is critical for avoiding penalties and maintaining reputation. Data science helps in monitoring compliance and identifying potential issues.

3.6 Inventory Management

Effective inventory management is crucial for minimizing costs and meeting customer demand. Data science optimizes inventory levels through predictive analytics and real-time monitoring.

- **Demand Forecasting**: Predictive models forecast demand for products, helping businesses maintain optimal inventory levels. This prevents stockouts and overstock situations.
- **Supply Chain Coordination**: Data science enhances coordination across the supply chain by providing real-time visibility into inventory levels and movement. This leads to improved efficiency and reduced costs.
- **Warehouse Optimization**: Analyzing warehouse operations data helps in optimizing layout, storage, and retrieval processes. This improves efficiency and reduces handling costs.

In conclusion, the importance of Data Science in today's world cannot be overstated. It drives decision-making, fuels innovation, and enhances operational efficiency, making it an indispensable tool for businesses across industries. As data continues to grow in volume and complexity, the role of data science will only become more critical, shaping the future of business and technology.

Operational Efficiency

Operational efficiency is a critical goal for any organization aiming to optimize performance, reduce costs, and improve productivity. Data Science plays a pivotal role in achieving this by leveraging data to streamline operations, automate processes, and enhance decision-making. This section explores how Data Science contributes to operational efficiency through various applications and methodologies.

1. Automation

Automation is a significant driver of operational efficiency, and Data Science is at the forefront of this revolution. By automating repetitive and mundane tasks, organizations can free up human resources for more strategic activities.

1.1 Robotic Process Automation (RPA)

Robotic Process Automation involves the use of software robots to automate routine tasks such as data entry, invoicing, and customer onboarding. RPA not only reduces the time required to perform these tasks but also minimizes human error, ensuring higher accuracy and efficiency.

- **Data Entry**: Automating data entry processes reduces manual errors and speeds up data processing. For example, banks use RPA to process loan applications, extracting and inputting data from forms automatically.
- **Invoice Processing**: RPA can handle invoice processing by extracting information from invoices, matching it with purchase orders, and entering it into accounting systems. This streamlines the accounts payable process and reduces processing time.
- **Customer Onboarding**: In industries like finance and telecom, RPA helps in automating the customer onboarding process by verifying documents, conducting background checks, and setting up accounts, thereby enhancing the customer experience.

1.2 Intelligent Automation

Intelligent Automation combines RPA with Artificial Intelligence (AI) and Machine Learning (ML) to handle more complex tasks that require cognitive capabilities. This advanced form of automation is capable of making decisions, learning from data, and adapting to new situations.

- **Customer Service**: AI-driven chatbots and virtual assistants provide 24/7 customer support, handling inquiries and resolving issues without human intervention. This not only improves customer satisfaction but also reduces the workload on human agents.
- **Fraud Detection**: Intelligent automation systems analyze transaction patterns to detect fraudulent activities in real-time. For example, credit card

companies use AI models to identify and block suspicious transactions automatically.

- **Supply Chain Optimization**: Intelligent automation optimizes supply chain operations by predicting demand, managing inventory, and coordinating logistics. AI models can suggest optimal routes for delivery trucks, reducing fuel costs and delivery times.

1.3 Workflow Optimization

Data Science helps organizations optimize their workflows by identifying inefficiencies and bottlenecks in business processes. By analyzing process data, companies can streamline operations and improve productivity.

- **Employee Performance**: Analyzing employee performance data helps in identifying areas for improvement and optimizing workforce allocation. For example, call centers use performance analytics to schedule shifts based on call volume predictions.
- **Production Processes**: In manufacturing, data science analyzes production line data to identify inefficiencies and optimize workflows. For instance, predictive maintenance models can schedule maintenance activities during non-peak hours, reducing downtime.
- **Document Management**: Automating document management processes, such as filing, retrieving, and sharing documents, improves efficiency and reduces the risk of errors. This is particularly important in sectors like healthcare and legal services where document handling is critical.

2. Resource Management

Efficient resource management is essential for maximizing productivity and minimizing waste. Data Science provides the tools needed to achieve optimal resource allocation and utilization.

2.1 Human Resources Management

Data Science plays a crucial role in managing human resources by analyzing employee data to optimize recruitment, performance, and retention strategies.

- **Recruitment**: Predictive analytics models analyze historical hiring data to identify the characteristics of successful employees. This helps in screening and selecting candidates who are more likely to perform well and stay with the company.
- **Performance Management**: Data-driven performance management systems track employee performance metrics and provide insights into areas for improvement. This helps in setting realistic goals, providing targeted training, and recognizing top performers.
- **Retention Strategies**: Predictive models identify employees at risk of leaving the organization by analyzing factors such as job satisfaction, engagement levels, and career progression. This enables HR teams to implement proactive retention strategies, such as personalized career development plans.

2.2 Asset Management

Effective management of physical assets is crucial for reducing operational costs and maximizing their lifespan. Data Science helps in monitoring and maintaining assets more efficiently.

- **Predictive Maintenance**: Predictive maintenance models analyze sensor data from equipment to predict potential failures before they occur. This allows for scheduled maintenance activities, reducing downtime and maintenance costs.
- **Inventory Optimization**: Data Science optimizes inventory management by predicting demand and adjusting stock levels accordingly. For example, retailers use demand forecasting models to ensure they have the right products in stock without overstocking.
- **Asset Utilization**: By analyzing usage patterns, organizations can optimize the utilization of their assets. For instance, transportation companies use telematics data to optimize fleet usage and reduce fuel consumption.

2.3 Energy Management

Data Science is instrumental in optimizing energy consumption, leading to cost savings and environmental benefits.

- **Smart Grids**: Smart grids use data analytics to monitor and manage electricity distribution in real-time. This ensures efficient energy use, reduces losses, and integrates renewable energy sources more effectively.
- **Building Management**: Data science optimizes energy use in buildings by analyzing data from

HVAC systems, lighting, and other utilities. Smart building systems adjust energy consumption based on occupancy patterns and external weather conditions.

- **Industrial Processes**: In industrial settings, data analytics optimize energy use in production processes. For example, predictive models can adjust machinery settings to minimize energy consumption while maintaining production efficiency.

3. Risk Management

Managing risk is crucial for the stability and growth of any organization. Data Science enhances risk management through predictive analytics and real-time monitoring.

3.1 Financial Risk Management

Financial institutions rely on Data Science to assess and mitigate various types of financial risk.

- **Credit Risk**: Predictive models analyze credit history, transaction data, and other factors to assess the creditworthiness of loan applicants. This helps banks make informed lending decisions and reduce default rates.
- **Market Risk**: Data Science models analyze market trends and economic indicators to predict potential market risks. This allows financial institutions to adjust their investment strategies and minimize losses.
- **Operational Risk**: Analyzing operational data helps in identifying and mitigating risks associated with internal processes, systems, and

human errors. For example, banks use data analytics to monitor compliance with regulatory requirements and prevent operational failures.

3.2 Operational Risk Management

Data Science helps organizations identify and mitigate operational risks across various domains.

- **Supply Chain Risks**: Predictive analytics models forecast potential supply chain disruptions due to factors like natural disasters, geopolitical events, or supplier issues. This enables companies to develop contingency plans and ensure business continuity.
- **Equipment Failure**: Predictive maintenance models analyze sensor data from machinery to predict equipment failures. This allows for proactive maintenance, reducing downtime and preventing costly breakdowns.
- **Compliance and Safety**: Data Science helps organizations monitor compliance with safety regulations and standards. For example, in the construction industry, analytics models analyze safety data to identify potential hazards and implement preventive measures.

3.3 Cybersecurity

In the digital age, cybersecurity is a critical concern for organizations. Data Science plays a key role in enhancing cybersecurity through anomaly detection and threat prediction.

- **Anomaly Detection**: Machine learning models analyze network traffic to detect unusual patterns that may indicate a cyber attack. For example, sudden spikes in data transfer or unusual login activities can trigger alerts for further investigation.

- **Threat Prediction**: Predictive analytics models identify potential threats by analyzing historical attack data and emerging threat patterns. This helps organizations implement preventive measures and strengthen their security posture.
- **Incident Response**: Data Science aids in the incident response process by analyzing attack patterns and determining the source and impact of a breach. This enables quicker resolution and minimizes damage.

4. Cost Reduction

Reducing operational costs is a primary objective for businesses aiming to improve their bottom line. Data Science helps organizations identify cost-saving opportunities and implement efficient practices.

4.1 Supply Chain Optimization

Optimizing supply chain operations through data analytics leads to significant cost savings.

- **Demand Forecasting**: Predictive models forecast demand for products, helping businesses maintain optimal inventory levels. This prevents overstocking and stockouts, reducing inventory carrying costs and lost sales.
- **Logistics Efficiency**: Data Science optimizes logistics by analyzing transportation data to identify the most efficient routes and modes of

delivery. This reduces fuel consumption, delivery times, and transportation costs.

- **Procurement Strategies**: Analyzing procurement data helps organizations identify cost-saving opportunities in supplier selection, contract negotiation, and purchasing practices. For example, companies can use spend analysis to consolidate purchases and negotiate better terms with suppliers.

4.2 Operational Efficiency

Streamlining operations through data-driven insights leads to cost savings and improved productivity.

- **Process Automation**: Automating routine tasks reduces labor costs and increases efficiency. For example, automating invoice processing reduces the need for manual data entry, speeding up the accounts payable process.
- **Workflow Optimization**: Analyzing workflow data helps identify inefficiencies and optimize business processes. For instance, lean manufacturing principles combined with data analytics can reduce waste and improve production efficiency.
- **Resource Allocation**: Data Science optimizes resource allocation by predicting demand and adjusting staffing levels accordingly. For example, call centers use predictive models to schedule shifts based on call volume forecasts, reducing labor costs.

4.3 Energy Savings

Optimizing energy consumption leads to significant cost savings and environmental benefits.

- **Smart Energy Management**: Data Science enables smart energy management systems that monitor and control energy use in real-time. For example, smart thermostats adjust heating and cooling settings based on occupancy and weather conditions, reducing energy costs.
- **Industrial Energy Efficiency**: Analyzing energy consumption data in industrial processes helps identify inefficiencies and implement energy-saving measures. For instance, optimizing machine settings can reduce energy use without compromising production output.
- **Renewable Energy Integration**: Data Science helps integrate renewable energy sources into the grid more effectively. Predictive models forecast energy production from solar and wind sources, allowing for better planning and utilization.

5. Quality Control

Maintaining high-quality standards is essential for customer satisfaction and business success. Data Science enhances quality control through advanced analytics and real-time monitoring.

5.1 Manufacturing Quality

In manufacturing, maintaining product quality is crucial for customer satisfaction and regulatory compliance. Data Science helps in monitoring and controlling quality throughout the production process.

- **Defect Detection**: Machine learning models analyze production data to detect defects and anomalies in real-time. This allows for immediate corrective actions, reducing the number of defective products and ensuring high-quality standards.
- **Process Control**: Statistical process control (SPC) techniques combined with data analytics monitor production processes to ensure they stay within predefined quality limits. For example, analyzing temperature and pressure data in real-time helps maintain optimal conditions for product manufacturing.
- **Supplier Quality Management**: Data Science helps in monitoring the quality of raw materials supplied by vendors. By analyzing supplier performance data, companies can identify reliable suppliers and negotiate better terms.

5.2 Service Quality

In service industries, maintaining high service quality is critical for customer retention and competitive advantage. Data Science provides insights into service performance and customer satisfaction.

- **Customer Feedback Analysis**: Analyzing customer feedback and reviews helps in identifying areas for improvement. For example, sentiment analysis of social media comments provides insights into customer perceptions and experiences.
- **Service Performance Metrics**: Monitoring key performance indicators (KPIs) such as response time, resolution time, and customer satisfaction scores helps in maintaining high service

standards. Data-driven insights enable service managers to address issues promptly and improve service quality.

- **Personalized Service**: Data Science enables personalized service experiences by analyzing customer data and preferences. For instance, recommendation systems in online platforms suggest products and services based on individual customer profiles.

5.3 Compliance

Ensuring compliance with regulations and standards is critical for avoiding penalties and maintaining reputation. Data Science helps organizations monitor compliance and identify potential issues.

- **Regulatory Compliance**: Analyzing compliance data helps organizations ensure they meet regulatory requirements. For example, financial institutions use data analytics to monitor transactions and detect potential money laundering activities.
- **Safety Standards**: In industries such as healthcare and manufacturing, maintaining safety standards is crucial. Data Science helps in monitoring safety data and identifying potential hazards, ensuring compliance with safety regulations.
- **Audit and Reporting**: Data-driven audit and reporting systems provide accurate and timely information for regulatory audits. This reduces the risk of non-compliance and ensures transparency in business operations.

6. Inventory Management

Effective inventory management is essential for minimizing costs and meeting customer demand. Data Science optimizes inventory levels through predictive analytics and real-time monitoring.

6.1 Demand Forecasting

Accurate demand forecasting is crucial for maintaining optimal inventory levels. Data Science models analyze historical sales data, market trends, and other factors to predict future demand.

- **Seasonal Trends**: Predictive models account for seasonal variations in demand, helping businesses stock up on popular items during peak seasons and reduce inventory during off-peak periods.
- **Market Conditions**: Analyzing market conditions and consumer behavior provides insights into potential demand shifts. For example, economic indicators and competitor activities can influence demand for certain products.
- **Promotional Impact**: Data Science helps in predicting the impact of promotional activities on demand. This enables businesses to adjust inventory levels and avoid stockouts or overstock situations.

6.2 Inventory Optimization

Optimizing inventory levels involves balancing the cost of holding inventory with the need to meet customer demand. Data Science provides the tools needed to achieve this balance.

- **Safety Stock**: Predictive models calculate optimal safety stock levels to buffer against uncertainties in demand and supply. This ensures that businesses can meet customer demand without incurring excessive holding costs.
- **Reorder Points**: Data Science determines optimal reorder points based on demand forecasts and lead times. This helps in maintaining inventory levels and preventing stockouts.
- **Inventory Turnover**: Analyzing inventory turnover ratios helps in identifying slow-moving and fast-moving items. This enables businesses to make informed decisions about purchasing, stocking, and pricing strategies.

6.3 Supply Chain Coordination

Effective supply chain coordination is essential for optimizing inventory management. Data Science enhances visibility and collaboration across the supply chain.

- **Real-Time Monitoring**: Real-time monitoring systems provide visibility into inventory levels and movement across the supply chain. This enables businesses to respond quickly to changes in demand and supply conditions.
- **Supplier Collaboration**: Data-driven insights enhance collaboration with suppliers, ensuring timely deliveries and reducing lead times. For example, sharing demand forecasts with suppliers helps in synchronizing production and delivery schedules.
- **Logistics Optimization**: Data Science optimizes logistics operations by analyzing transportation data to identify the most efficient routes and

modes of delivery. This reduces transportation costs and improves delivery times.

6.4 Warehouse Management

Efficient warehouse management is crucial for optimizing inventory storage and retrieval processes. Data Science provides insights into warehouse operations and helps in improving efficiency.

- **Layout Optimization**: Analyzing warehouse layout data helps in optimizing storage space and reducing retrieval times. For example, frequently picked items can be stored closer to the shipping area to speed up order fulfillment.
- **Inventory Tracking**: Real-time inventory tracking systems provide accurate information about inventory levels and locations within the warehouse. This reduces the risk of stockouts and overstock situations.
- **Order Fulfillment**: Data Science optimizes order fulfillment processes by analyzing order data and warehouse operations. For example, batch picking strategies can reduce the time required to pick and pack orders, improving overall efficiency.

In conclusion, Data Science is a powerful tool for enhancing operational efficiency across various domains. By leveraging data-driven insights, organizations can automate processes, optimize resource management, manage risks effectively, reduce costs, maintain high-quality standards, and manage inventory efficiently. As data continues to grow in volume and complexity, the role of Data Science in driving operational efficiency will only become more critical, shaping the future of business and industry.

Data Science Tools and Technologies

Data Science relies on a wide array of tools and technologies to process, analyze, and interpret large volumes of data. These tools help data scientists to clean data, build models, visualize results, and derive actionable insights. This section provides an in-depth look at some of the most important tools and technologies in the field of Data Science, including programming languages, frameworks, and platforms.

1. Programming Languages

Programming languages are the backbone of Data Science, providing the means to manipulate data, perform statistical analyses, and build machine learning models. The most commonly used languages in Data Science are Python, R, SQL, and Julia.

1.1 Python

Python is the most popular programming language for Data Science due to its simplicity, readability, and extensive library support. It is widely used for data manipulation, statistical analysis, machine learning, and data visualization.

- **Pandas**: Pandas is a powerful data manipulation library that provides data structures and functions needed to clean and manipulate data. It is particularly useful for handling large datasets and performing complex data operations.

- **NumPy**: NumPy is the foundational package for numerical computing in Python. It provides support for arrays, matrices, and numerous mathematical functions, making it essential for performing numerical computations and data analysis.
- **Scikit-learn**: Scikit-learn is a popular machine learning library that provides simple and efficient tools for data mining and data analysis. It includes algorithms for classification, regression, clustering, and dimensionality reduction.
- **Matplotlib**: Matplotlib is a plotting library that allows for the creation of static, interactive, and animated visualizations. It is widely used for generating plots, histograms, and other graphical representations of data.

1.2 R

R is another widely used programming language in Data Science, particularly for statistical analysis and data visualization. It is favored by statisticians and data analysts for its robust statistical capabilities and graphical libraries.

- **ggplot2**: ggplot2 is a powerful data visualization package in R, known for its ability to create complex and aesthetically pleasing plots. It is based on the grammar of graphics, allowing for flexible and layered visualizations.
- **dplyr**: dplyr is a data manipulation package in R that provides a set of functions for data transformation. It is designed to work with data frames and is optimized for performance, making it suitable for handling large datasets.

- **caret**: caret is a package in R that streamlines the process of building predictive models. It provides functions for data splitting, pre-processing, model tuning, and evaluation, supporting a wide range of machine learning algorithms.
- **Shiny**: Shiny is a web application framework for R that allows data scientists to build interactive web applications directly from R scripts. It is commonly used for creating dashboards and data visualization tools.

1.3 SQL

SQL (Structured Query Language) is essential for managing and querying relational databases. It is used to extract and manipulate data stored in databases, making it a critical skill for data scientists.

- **MySQL**: MySQL is an open-source relational database management system that is widely used for web applications and data warehousing. It supports SQL for data manipulation and is known for its reliability and performance.
- **PostgreSQL**: PostgreSQL is an advanced, open-source relational database that supports both SQL and NoSQL queries. It is known for its extensibility and support for complex queries, making it suitable for a wide range of applications.
- **SQLite**: SQLite is a lightweight, serverless database engine that is widely used for embedded applications. It supports most SQL features and is easy to set up and use, making it ideal for small to medium-sized projects.
- **Microsoft SQL Server**: Microsoft SQL Server is a relational database management system

developed by Microsoft. It supports SQL for data manipulation and provides advanced features such as data warehousing, analytics, and business intelligence tools.

1.4 Julia

Julia is a high-level, high-performance programming language for technical computing, with syntax that is familiar to users of other technical computing environments.

- **DataFrames.jl**: DataFrames.jl is a package in Julia that provides data manipulation tools similar to those in Pandas for Python and dplyr for R. It is optimized for performance and ease of use.
- **Flux.jl**: Flux.jl is a machine learning library in Julia that is designed to be flexible and easy to use. It supports a wide range of machine learning models and is integrated with Julia's high-performance capabilities.
- **Plots.jl**: Plots.jl is a powerful plotting package in Julia that supports multiple backends for creating static, interactive, and animated plots. It is designed to be easy to use while providing extensive customization options.
- **JuMP**: JuMP is a domain-specific modeling language for mathematical optimization embedded in Julia. It is used for solving optimization problems and is known for its speed and ease of use.

2. Data Manipulation and Cleaning Tools

Data manipulation and cleaning are crucial steps in the Data Science process. These tools help in transforming raw data into a structured format suitable for analysis.

2.1 Pandas

Pandas is a Python library that provides data structures and functions for data manipulation and analysis. It is particularly useful for handling tabular data and time series.

- **DataFrames**: Pandas DataFrames are two-dimensional, size-mutable, and potentially heterogeneous tabular data structures. They allow for the easy manipulation of data, including filtering, grouping, and aggregation.
- **Series**: Pandas Series are one-dimensional labeled arrays capable of holding any data type. They are used for handling and manipulating single columns or rows of data.
- **Data Cleaning**: Pandas provides functions for handling missing data, removing duplicates, and transforming data types. It simplifies the process of preparing data for analysis.

2.2 dplyr

dplyr is an R package that provides a grammar for data manipulation. It simplifies the process of transforming and summarizing data.

- **Data Manipulation Verbs**: dplyr introduces a set of verbs, such as select, filter, mutate, summarize, and arrange, which make data manipulation tasks more intuitive and readable.

- **Pipelines**: dplyr supports pipelines, allowing for the chaining of multiple data manipulation operations in a concise and readable manner.
- **Data Transformation**: dplyr provides functions for transforming data, including reshaping, merging, and grouping, making it easier to prepare data for analysis.

2.3 SQL

SQL is used for querying and manipulating data stored in relational databases. It is essential for extracting data and performing complex queries.

- **SELECT Statements**: SQL SELECT statements are used to query data from databases. They support various clauses, such as WHERE, GROUP BY, and ORDER BY, to filter and organize data.
- **Joins**: SQL supports different types of joins (INNER JOIN, LEFT JOIN, RIGHT JOIN, FULL OUTER JOIN) to combine data from multiple tables based on a related column.
- **Data Aggregation**: SQL provides functions for aggregating data, such as COUNT, SUM, AVG, MIN, and MAX. These functions are useful for summarizing data and deriving insights.

2.4 Apache Spark

Apache Spark is a unified analytics engine for large-scale data processing. It provides an interface for programming entire clusters with implicit data parallelism and fault tolerance.

- **DataFrame API**: Spark's DataFrame API provides high-level abstractions for data manipulation, similar to those in Pandas and dplyr. It supports operations such as filtering, grouping, and joining.
- **Spark SQL**: Spark SQL allows for querying structured data using SQL syntax. It integrates with Spark's core engine, enabling the execution of complex queries on large datasets.
- **Machine Learning**: Spark's MLlib provides scalable machine learning algorithms for classification, regression, clustering, and collaborative filtering.

3. Data Visualization Tools

Data visualization is essential for interpreting data and communicating insights effectively. These tools help in creating charts, graphs, and other visual representations of data.

3.1 Matplotlib

Matplotlib is a comprehensive library for creating static, animated, and interactive visualizations in Python.

- **Line Plots**: Matplotlib can create line plots to visualize data trends over time or other continuous variables. Line plots are useful for time series analysis and trend visualization.
- **Bar Charts**: Bar charts are used to compare categorical data. Matplotlib provides functions to create both vertical and horizontal bar charts, making it easy to compare different categories.
- **Histograms**: Histograms are used to visualize the distribution of data. Matplotlib's histogram

functions allow for the creation of detailed and customizable histograms.

3.2 ggplot2

ggplot2 is an R package that implements the grammar of graphics, providing a powerful and flexible system for creating complex visualizations.

- **Layered Graphics**: ggplot2 allows for the layering of multiple graphical elements, such as points, lines, and bars, to create complex and informative visualizations.
- **Faceting**: Faceting is a technique in ggplot2 that allows for the creation of multiple plots based on subsets of the data. This is useful for comparing different groups or categories.
- **Themes**: ggplot2 provides a range of themes and customization options to enhance the appearance of plots. Users can modify colors, fonts, and other graphical elements to create visually appealing charts.

3.3 Tableau

Tableau is a powerful data visualization tool that enables users to create interactive and shareable dashboards.

- **Interactive Dashboards**: Tableau allows users to create interactive dashboards that enable exploration and analysis of data through filters, highlights, and drill-downs.
- **Data Connectivity**: Tableau supports connectivity to various data sources, including spreadsheets, databases, and cloud services. This

enables the integration and analysis of data from multiple sources.

- **Storytelling**: Tableau provides features for creating data stories, which are sequences of visualizations that convey insights and findings in a narrative format.

3.4 Power BI

Power BI is a business analytics service by Microsoft that provides interactive visualizations and business intelligence capabilities.

- **Data Integration**: Power BI supports integration with a wide range of data sources, including Excel, SQL Server, and Azure. This enables the creation of comprehensive and integrated dashboards.
- **Custom Visualizations**: Power BI provides a gallery of custom visualizations, allowing users to create unique and tailored visualizations for their data.
- **Collaboration**: Power BI facilitates collaboration by allowing users to share dashboards and reports with colleagues and stakeholders. This enables real-time collaboration and decision-making.

3.5 D3.js

D3.js is a JavaScript library for producing dynamic, interactive data visualizations in web browsers.

- **SVG Manipulation**: D3.js allows for the manipulation of SVG elements to create complex and interactive visualizations. This provides extensive customization and control over the appearance of visualizations.

- **Data Binding**: D3.js supports data binding, which allows for the automatic updating of visualizations based on changes in the underlying data.
- **Interactivity**: D3.js provides features for creating interactive visualizations, such as tooltips, hover effects, and animations. This enhances the user experience and facilitates data exploration.

4. Machine Learning and AI Frameworks

Machine learning and AI frameworks provide tools and libraries for building, training, and deploying machine learning models.

4.1 TensorFlow

TensorFlow is an open-source machine learning framework developed by Google. It provides a comprehensive ecosystem for building and deploying machine learning models.

- **Keras**: Keras is a high-level API for building and training deep learning models. It is integrated with TensorFlow and simplifies the process of building neural networks.
- **TensorFlow Extended (TFX)**: TFX is an end-to-end platform for deploying production machine learning pipelines. It includes components for data validation, model training, and model serving.
- **TensorFlow Lite**: TensorFlow Lite is a framework for deploying machine learning models on mobile and embedded devices. It

provides tools for optimizing models for low-latency and resource-constrained environments.

4.2 PyTorch

PyTorch is an open-source machine learning framework developed by Facebook. It is known for its dynamic computation graph and ease of use.

- **TorchScript**: TorchScript is an intermediate representation of PyTorch models that enables them to be optimized and run in production environments. It allows for the seamless transition from research to production.
- **ONNX (Open Neural Network Exchange)**: ONNX is an open format for representing machine learning models. PyTorch supports exporting models to ONNX, enabling interoperability with other frameworks and tools.
- **AutoGrad**: AutoGrad is PyTorch's automatic differentiation library, which simplifies the process of computing gradients for optimizing machine learning models.

4.3 Scikit-learn

Scikit-learn is a Python library that provides simple and efficient tools for data mining and data analysis. It is built on NumPy, SciPy, and matplotlib.

- **Supervised Learning**: Scikit-learn provides a wide range of supervised learning algorithms, including linear regression, logistic regression, support vector machines, and random forests.
- **Unsupervised Learning**: Scikit-learn includes algorithms for unsupervised learning, such as k-

means clustering, hierarchical clustering, and principal component analysis (PCA).

- **Model Evaluation**: Scikit-learn provides tools for model evaluation and validation, including cross-validation, grid search, and metrics for measuring model performance.

4.4 XGBoost

XGBoost (Extreme Gradient Boosting) is an optimized gradient boosting library designed for speed and performance. It is widely used in machine learning competitions and real-world applications.

- **Tree-based Models**: XGBoost provides efficient implementations of tree-based models, which are known for their high predictive performance and ability to handle large datasets.
- **Regularization**: XGBoost includes built-in regularization techniques to prevent overfitting and improve model generalization.
- **Distributed Computing**: XGBoost supports distributed computing, enabling the training of models on large datasets across multiple machines.

4.5 H2O.ai

H2O.ai is an open-source platform for building and deploying machine learning models. It provides tools for both supervised and unsupervised learning.

- **AutoML**: H2O.ai's AutoML automates the process of training and tuning machine learning models. It includes features for model selection, hyperparameter tuning, and ensemble learning.

- **Distributed Computing**: H2O.ai supports distributed computing, allowing for the training of models on large datasets across multiple nodes.
- **Integration**: H2O.ai integrates with various data science tools and platforms, including Python, R, and Apache Spark, enabling seamless workflows and interoperability.

5. Big Data Platforms

Big Data platforms provide the infrastructure and tools needed to store, process, and analyze large volumes of data.

5.1 Apache Hadoop

Apache Hadoop is an open-source framework for distributed storage and processing of large datasets. It consists of several components, including HDFS, MapReduce, and YARN.

- **HDFS (Hadoop Distributed File System)**: HDFS is a distributed file system that provides high-throughput access to data. It is designed to store large datasets across multiple nodes.
- **MapReduce**: MapReduce is a programming model for processing large datasets in parallel. It divides tasks into smaller sub-tasks, which are processed simultaneously across multiple nodes.
- **YARN (Yet Another Resource Negotiator)**: YARN is a resource management layer in Hadoop that allocates system resources to various applications running on the Hadoop cluster.

5.2 Apache Spark

Apache Spark is a unified analytics engine for large-scale data processing. It provides an interface for programming entire clusters with implicit data parallelism and fault tolerance.

- **Spark Core**: Spark Core is the foundation of the Apache Spark framework. It provides basic functionalities for task scheduling, memory management, fault recovery, and interacting with storage systems.
- **Spark SQL**: Spark SQL is a module for working with structured data. It provides a programming abstraction called DataFrames and allows for the execution of SQL queries.
- **Spark Streaming**: Spark Streaming is a module for processing real-time data streams. It supports scalable, high-throughput, and fault-tolerant stream processing.
- **MLlib**: MLlib is Spark's machine learning library, providing scalable machine learning algorithms for classification, regression, clustering, and collaborative filtering.

5.3 Apache Kafka

Apache Kafka is a distributed streaming platform that allows for the real-time processing of data streams. It is designed to handle high-throughput, fault-tolerant, and scalable data streams.

- **Producers and Consumers**: Kafka producers publish data to Kafka topics, while consumers subscribe to these topics to read the data. This decouples data producers and consumers, enabling scalable and flexible data processing.

- **Kafka Streams**: Kafka Streams is a stream processing library built on top of Apache Kafka. It allows for the development of real-time applications that process and analyze data streams.
- **Connect API**: Kafka Connect is a framework for connecting Kafka with external systems, such as databases, key-value stores, and search indexes. It provides pre-built connectors for various data sources and sinks.

5.4 Google BigQuery

Google BigQuery is a fully managed, serverless data warehouse that enables fast SQL queries using the processing power of Google's infrastructure.

- **Scalable Storage**: BigQuery provides scalable and high-performance storage for large datasets. It automatically manages the underlying infrastructure, allowing users to focus on data analysis.
- **SQL Queries**: BigQuery supports standard SQL for querying and analyzing data. It provides features such as nested and repeated fields, allowing for the handling of complex data structures.
- **Integration**: BigQuery integrates with various Google Cloud services, including Google Cloud Storage, Dataflow, and AI Platform, enabling seamless data workflows and analytics.

5.5 Amazon Redshift

Amazon Redshift is a fully managed data warehouse service in the cloud that enables fast and efficient querying of large datasets.

- **Columnar Storage**: Redshift uses columnar storage, which optimizes storage and query performance for analytical workloads. This allows for efficient data compression and retrieval.
- **Massively Parallel Processing (MPP)**: Redshift's architecture is based on massively parallel processing, allowing for the distribution of queries across multiple nodes for faster execution.
- **Integration**: Redshift integrates with various AWS services, including S3, Glue, and SageMaker, enabling comprehensive data processing and analytics workflows.

5.6 Azure Synapse Analytics

Azure Synapse Analytics is an integrated analytics service that accelerates time to insight across data warehouses and big data systems.

- **Unified Analytics**: Azure Synapse integrates big data and data warehousing into a single service, enabling seamless data integration, exploration, preparation, and analysis.
- **Synapse SQL**: Synapse SQL provides on-demand and provisioned query engines for data warehousing and big data analytics. It supports both T-SQL and SQL on-demand queries.
- **Spark Integration**: Azure Synapse integrates with Apache Spark, providing a powerful engine for big data processing and machine learning. It

enables the development of end-to-end data pipelines.

6. Cloud Platforms

Cloud platforms provide the infrastructure and services needed for scalable data storage, processing, and analysis.

6.1 Amazon Web Services (AWS)

AWS offers a comprehensive suite of cloud services for data science, including data storage, computing, machine learning, and analytics.

- **S3 (Simple Storage Service)**: S3 is an object storage service that provides scalable and durable storage for large datasets. It is commonly used for data lakes and backup storage.
- **EC2 (Elastic Compute Cloud)**: EC2 provides scalable computing capacity in the cloud. It allows users to run virtual servers for data processing and analysis.
- **SageMaker**: SageMaker is a fully managed machine learning service that provides tools for building, training, and deploying machine learning models. It supports popular frameworks such as TensorFlow, PyTorch, and scikit-learn.

6.2 Google Cloud Platform (GCP)

GCP provides a range of cloud services for data storage, processing, and machine learning.

- **BigQuery**: BigQuery is a fully managed, serverless data warehouse that enables fast and scalable SQL queries. It is designed for analyzing large datasets in real-time.

- **Compute Engine**: Compute Engine provides virtual machines for running custom computing workloads. It supports a wide range of configurations for different processing needs.
- **AI Platform**: AI Platform provides tools for building, training, and deploying machine learning models. It supports popular frameworks and integrates with other GCP services.

6.3 Microsoft Azure

Azure offers a comprehensive suite of cloud services for data storage, processing, and machine learning.

- **Azure Blob Storage**: Blob Storage is an object storage service for storing large amounts of unstructured data. It is commonly used for data lakes and backup storage.
- **Azure Virtual Machines**: Virtual Machines provide scalable computing capacity for running custom workloads. They support a wide range of configurations and operating systems.
- **Azure Machine Learning**: Azure Machine Learning is a cloud service for building, training, and deploying machine learning models. It provides tools for automated machine learning, model management, and deployment.

Conclusion

Data Science relies on a diverse set of tools and technologies to handle the complexities of data manipulation, analysis, and visualization. Programming languages like Python and R provide the foundation for data analysis and model building. Data manipulation tools like Pandas and dplyr streamline the process of cleaning and transforming data. Visualization tools like Matplotlib and Tableau help in interpreting data and communicating insights effectively. Machine learning frameworks like TensorFlow and PyTorch enable the development of sophisticated models, while big data platforms like Apache Hadoop and Google BigQuery handle large-scale data processing. Cloud platforms like AWS, GCP, and Azure provide the infrastructure needed for scalable and efficient data workflows. By leveraging these tools and technologies, data scientists can unlock the full potential of data and drive meaningful insights and decisions.

4o
Write the sub-points of above point number 5 in 3000 words as American English Please write in the English language. Please write in English language.
ChatGPT

5. Big Data Platforms

Big Data platforms provide the infrastructure and tools needed to store, process, and analyze large volumes of data. These platforms are essential for handling the massive amounts of data generated by modern organizations and enabling data-driven decision-making. In this section, we will explore some of the most prominent Big Data platforms and their key features.

1. Apache Hadoop

Apache Hadoop is an open-source framework for distributed storage and processing of large datasets. It revolutionized the way organizations handle Big Data by introducing a scalable and fault-tolerant architecture. The core components of Hadoop include:

1.1 HDFS (Hadoop Distributed File System): HDFS is a distributed file system that provides high-throughput access to data. It divides large files into smaller blocks and stores them across multiple nodes in a cluster, ensuring redundancy and fault tolerance.

1.2 MapReduce: MapReduce is a programming model for processing and analyzing large datasets in parallel. It divides tasks into smaller sub-tasks, which are executed simultaneously across multiple nodes in the Hadoop cluster. MapReduce is highly scalable and fault-tolerant, making it suitable for processing petabytes of data.

1.3 YARN (Yet Another Resource Negotiator): YARN is a resource management layer in Hadoop that manages resources and schedules tasks across the cluster. It allows multiple data processing frameworks, such as MapReduce, Spark, and Tez, to run concurrently on the same cluster, improving resource utilization and flexibility.

Apache Hadoop is widely used in industries such as finance, healthcare, e-commerce, and telecommunications for a variety of use cases, including log analysis, data warehousing, recommendation systems, and fraud detection.

2. Apache Spark

Apache Spark is a unified analytics engine for large-scale data processing. It provides an interface for programming entire clusters with implicit data parallelism and fault tolerance. Spark's architecture is designed to overcome the limitations of traditional MapReduce-based systems and offers several key advantages:

2.1 Spark Core: Spark Core is the foundation of the Apache Spark framework. It provides basic functionalities for task scheduling, memory management, fault recovery, and interacting with storage systems. Spark Core supports both batch and streaming data processing.

2.2 Spark SQL: Spark SQL is a module for working with structured data. It provides a programming abstraction called DataFrames, which allows for the execution of SQL queries and DataFrame operations on distributed datasets. Spark SQL enables seamless integration with existing SQL-based tools and libraries.

2.3 Spark Streaming: Spark Streaming is a module for processing real-time data streams. It ingests data from various sources, such as Kafka, Flume, and HDFS, and processes it in micro-batches or continuous streams. Spark Streaming provides high-throughput, fault-tolerant stream processing with exactly-once semantics.

2.4 MLlib: MLlib is Spark's machine learning library, providing scalable machine learning algorithms for classification, regression, clustering, and collaborative filtering. It is built on top of Spark Core and leverages Spark's distributed computing capabilities to train models on large datasets.

Apache Spark is widely adopted in industries such as advertising, finance, healthcare, and gaming for a range of use cases, including real-time analytics, recommendation systems, fraud detection, and predictive maintenance.

3. Apache Kafka

Apache Kafka is a distributed streaming platform that allows for the real-time processing of data streams. It is designed to handle high-throughput, fault-tolerant, and scalable data streams from various sources. Kafka's architecture consists of the following components:

3.1 Producers and Consumers: Kafka producers publish data to Kafka topics, while consumers subscribe to these topics to read the data. This decouples data producers and consumers, enabling scalable and flexible data processing pipelines.

3.2 Kafka Streams: Kafka Streams is a stream processing library built on top of Apache Kafka. It allows developers to build real-time applications that process and analyze data streams directly within the Kafka ecosystem. Kafka Streams provides stateful processing, windowing, and fault tolerance features.

3.3 Connect API: Kafka Connect is a framework for connecting Kafka with external systems, such as databases, key-value stores, and search indexes. It provides pre-built connectors for various data sources and sinks, allowing for seamless integration with existing data infrastructure.

Apache Kafka is widely used for real-time data processing use cases such as event streaming, log aggregation, clickstream analysis, and IoT telemetry. It is employed by companies across industries such as retail, telecommunications, financial services, and social media.

4. Google BigQuery

Google BigQuery is a fully managed, serverless data warehouse that enables fast SQL queries using the processing power of Google's infrastructure. It offers several key features:

4.1 Scalable Storage: BigQuery provides scalable and high-performance storage for large datasets. It automatically manages the underlying infrastructure, allowing users to focus on data analysis rather than infrastructure management.

4.2 SQL Queries: BigQuery supports standard SQL for querying and analyzing data. It provides features such as nested and repeated fields, allowing for the handling of complex data structures. BigQuery's query engine is highly parallelized and optimized for interactive analysis of large datasets.

4.3 Integration: BigQuery integrates with various Google Cloud services, including Google Cloud Storage, Dataflow, and AI Platform. This enables comprehensive data processing and analytics workflows, from data ingestion to model training and deployment.

Google BigQuery is widely used for analytical use cases such as business intelligence, data warehousing, ad hoc analysis, and predictive analytics. It is popular among enterprises and startups alike for its scalability, performance, and ease of use.

5. Amazon Redshift

Amazon Redshift is a fully managed data warehouse service in the cloud that enables fast and efficient querying of large datasets. It offers the following key features:

5.1 Columnar Storage: Redshift uses columnar storage, which optimizes storage and query performance for analytical workloads. This allows for efficient data compression and retrieval, resulting in faster query execution times.

5.2 Massively Parallel Processing (MPP): Redshift's architecture is based on massively parallel processing, allowing for the distribution of queries across multiple nodes for faster execution. Redshift automatically scales compute and storage resources based on workload demands, ensuring consistent performance.

5.3 Integration: Redshift integrates with various AWS services, including S3, Glue, and SageMaker, enabling comprehensive data processing and analytics workflows. It also supports integration with third-party BI tools and data visualization platforms, allowing users to leverage existing tools and workflows.

Amazon Redshift is widely used for data warehousing, business intelligence, reporting, and ad hoc analysis. It is favored by organizations across industries such as retail, healthcare, finance, and gaming for its scalability, performance, and ease of management.

6. Azure Synapse Analytics

Azure Synapse Analytics is an integrated analytics service that accelerates time to insight across data warehouses and big data systems. It offers the following key capabilities:

6.1 Unified Analytics: Azure Synapse integrates big data and data warehousing into a single service, enabling seamless data integration, exploration, preparation, and analysis. It provides a unified environment for querying and processing structured and unstructured data.

6.2 Synapse SQL: Synapse SQL provides on-demand and provisioned query engines for data warehousing and big data analytics. It supports both T-SQL and SQL on-demand queries, allowing users to analyze data at scale with familiar tools and languages.

6.3 Spark Integration: Azure Synapse integrates with Apache Spark, providing a powerful engine for big data processing and machine learning. It enables the development of end-to-end data pipelines for data preparation, analysis, and model training.

Azure Synapse Analytics is widely used for analytical use cases such as data warehousing, business intelligence, predictive analytics, and machine learning. It is adopted by organizations across industries such as manufacturing, finance, healthcare, and government for its scalability, performance, and enterprise-grade security.

Conclusion

Big Data platforms play a crucial role in enabling organizations to store, process, and analyze large volumes of data efficiently. Apache Hadoop revolutionized the field with its distributed storage and processing capabilities, while Apache Spark introduced a unified analytics engine for large-scale data processing. Apache Kafka enables real-time data processing and event streaming, while Google BigQuery and Amazon

Redshift offer fully managed data warehouse solutions in the cloud. Azure Synapse Analytics integrates big data and data warehousing into a single service, providing a unified environment for data analytics. By leveraging these Big Data platforms, organizations can unlock valuable insights from their data and gain a competitive edge in today's data-driven world.

6. Cloud Platforms

Cloud platforms provide the infrastructure and services needed for scalable data storage, processing, and analysis. They offer a range of tools and services that enable organizations to leverage the power of the cloud for their data needs. In this section, we will explore some of the leading cloud platforms and their key features.

1. Amazon Web Services (AWS)

Amazon Web Services (AWS) is a comprehensive cloud computing platform provided by Amazon. It offers a wide range of services for data storage, processing, and analysis. Some of the key features of AWS include:

1.1 Amazon S3 (Simple Storage Service): Amazon S3 is an object storage service that provides scalable storage for data of any size. It is highly durable and designed to store and retrieve large datasets with high availability and low latency.

1.2 Amazon EC2 (Elastic Compute Cloud): Amazon EC2 is a web service that provides resizable compute capacity in the cloud. It allows users to launch virtual servers (instances) on-demand, enabling them to run applications and workloads of any size.

1.3 Amazon SageMaker: Amazon SageMaker is a fully managed machine learning service that enables developers to build, train, and deploy machine learning models at scale. It provides tools for data labeling, model training, and model deployment, making it easy to develop and deploy machine learning applications.

AWS is widely used by organizations of all sizes for a variety of use cases, including data warehousing, analytics, machine learning, and IoT. Its scalability, reliability, and extensive set of services make it a popular choice for cloud-based data solutions.

2. Google Cloud Platform (GCP)

Google Cloud Platform (GCP) is a suite of cloud computing services provided by Google. It offers a wide range of services for data storage, processing, and analysis. Some of the key features of GCP include:

2.1 BigQuery: BigQuery is a fully managed, serverless data warehouse that enables fast SQL queries using Google's infrastructure. It allows users to analyze large datasets quickly and easily, making it ideal for business intelligence, data warehousing, and ad hoc analysis.

2.2 Compute Engine: Compute Engine is a service that provides virtual machines for running applications and workloads in the cloud. It offers customizable virtual machines with flexible configurations, allowing users to choose the resources that best fit their needs.

2.3 AI Platform: AI Platform is a suite of machine learning services that enables developers to build, train, and deploy machine learning models at scale. It provides tools for data preprocessing, model training, and model serving, making it easy to develop and deploy machine learning applications.

GCP is used by organizations across industries for a variety of use cases, including data analytics, machine learning, and IoT. Its reliability, performance, and extensive set of services make it a popular choice for cloud-based data solutions.

3. Microsoft Azure

Microsoft Azure is a cloud computing platform provided by Microsoft. It offers a wide range of services for data storage, processing, and analysis. Some of the key features of Azure include:

3.1 Azure Blob Storage: Azure Blob Storage is a scalable object storage service that allows users to store and retrieve large amounts of unstructured data. It is highly durable and designed to handle data of any size with high availability and low latency.

3.2 Azure Virtual Machines: Azure Virtual Machines are resizable compute instances that allow users to run applications and workloads in the cloud. They offer a wide range of configurations and operating systems, making it easy to deploy and manage virtual machines for various use cases.

3.3 Azure Machine Learning: Azure Machine Learning is a fully managed machine learning service that enables developers to build, train, and deploy machine learning models at scale. It provides tools for data labeling, model training, and model deployment, making it easy to develop and deploy machine learning applications.

Azure is used by organizations of all sizes for a variety of use cases, including data analytics, machine learning, and IoT. Its reliability, performance, and extensive set of services make it a popular choice for cloud-based data solutions.

Conclusion

Cloud platforms play a crucial role in enabling organizations to leverage the power of the cloud for their data needs. Whether it's storing and processing large volumes of data or building and deploying machine learning models, cloud platforms offer a wide range of services and tools to meet the needs of modern businesses. By leveraging the scalability, reliability, and flexibility of cloud platforms, organizations can unlock valuable insights from their data and gain a competitive edge in today's data-driven world.

7. Data Science Tools and Libraries

Data science tools and libraries are essential for performing various tasks in data analysis, machine learning, and visualization. These tools provide developers and data scientists with the necessary functionalities to explore data, build models, and derive insights. In this section, we will explore some of the most widely used data science tools and libraries and their key features.

1. Python

Python is a versatile programming language that is widely used in data science for its simplicity, readability, and extensive ecosystem of libraries. Some of the key data science libraries in Python include:

1.1 NumPy: NumPy is a fundamental package for numerical computing in Python. It provides support for large, multi-dimensional arrays and matrices, along with a collection of mathematical functions to operate on these arrays efficiently.

1.2 Pandas: Pandas is a powerful data manipulation and analysis library for Python. It provides data structures like DataFrame and Series, which allow users to easily manipulate and analyze tabular data, including data cleaning, filtering, and aggregation.

1.3 Matplotlib: Matplotlib is a comprehensive library for creating static, interactive, and animated visualizations in Python. It provides a wide range of plotting functions for creating line plots, scatter plots, bar charts, histograms, and more.

1.4 Scikit-learn: Scikit-learn is a popular machine learning library for Python. It provides simple and efficient tools for data mining and data analysis, including classification, regression, clustering, dimensionality reduction, and model evaluation.

Python's rich ecosystem of libraries makes it a preferred choice for data scientists and developers for a wide range of data science tasks, from data exploration to model building and visualization.

2. R

R is a programming language and environment specifically designed for statistical computing and graphics. It is widely used in academia and industry for data analysis, statistical modeling, and visualization. Some of the key data science packages in R include:

2.1 dplyr: dplyr is a powerful data manipulation package for R. It provides a set of functions for filtering, sorting, summarizing, and mutating data, allowing users to perform complex data manipulation tasks easily and efficiently.

2.2 ggplot2: ggplot2 is a popular data visualization package for R. It provides a flexible and powerful system for creating static and interactive visualizations, including scatter plots, line plots, bar charts, histograms, and more.

2.3 caret: caret is a comprehensive package for machine learning in R. It provides a unified interface for training and evaluating machine learning models, as well as tools for data preprocessing, feature selection, and model tuning.

R's extensive collection of packages makes it a powerful tool for data analysis and visualization. Its rich statistical capabilities and expressive syntax make it particularly well-suited for exploratory data analysis and statistical modeling.

3. SQL

SQL (Structured Query Language) is a standard language for managing and manipulating relational databases. It is widely used in data science for querying and analyzing structured data. Some of the key features of SQL include:

3.1 Data Querying: SQL provides powerful querying capabilities for selecting, filtering, sorting, and aggregating data from databases. It supports a wide range of operators and functions for manipulating and transforming data.

3.2 Data Manipulation: SQL allows users to perform various data manipulation tasks, such as inserting, updating, and deleting data from databases. It also supports transactions for ensuring data integrity and consistency.

3.3 Data Analysis: SQL provides tools for performing data analysis and statistical calculations directly within the database. It supports aggregate functions like SUM, AVG, COUNT, and GROUP BY for summarizing and aggregating data.

SQL is an essential skill for data scientists and analysts working with relational databases. Its simplicity, versatility, and widespread adoption make it a valuable tool for querying and analyzing data in a variety of industries and applications.

4. Tableau

Tableau is a powerful data visualization tool that allows users to create interactive and insightful dashboards and reports. Some of the key features of Tableau include:

4.1 Drag-and-Drop Interface: Tableau provides an intuitive drag-and-drop interface for creating visualizations. Users can easily connect to data sources, drag fields onto the canvas, and create visualizations with a few clicks.

4.2 Interactive Visualizations: Tableau allows users to create interactive visualizations that enable exploration and analysis of data. Users can filter, drill down, and highlight data points to uncover insights and trends.

4.3 Dashboarding: Tableau enables users to combine multiple visualizations into interactive dashboards. Dashboards provide a holistic view of the data and allow users to monitor key metrics and KPIs in real-time.

Tableau's user-friendly interface and powerful visualization capabilities make it a popular choice for data analysts, business intelligence professionals, and decision-makers looking to derive insights from their data.

5. Jupyter Notebooks

Jupyter Notebooks is an open-source web application that allows users to create and share documents containing live code, equations, visualizations, and narrative text. Some of the key features of Jupyter Notebooks include:

5.1 Interactive Computing: Jupyter Notebooks supports interactive computing with support for multiple programming languages, including Python, R, and Julia. Users can write and execute code in cells, view the output, and iterate on their analyses in real-time.

5.2 Rich Text Support: Jupyter Notebooks support rich text formatting with support for Markdown, LaTeX, and HTML. Users can add headings, lists, tables, equations, and hyperlinks to their notebooks to provide context and documentation for their analyses.

5.3 Visualizations: Jupyter Notebooks support inline plotting with support for various plotting libraries, including Matplotlib, Seaborn, and Plotly. Users can create interactive visualizations directly within their notebooks to explore and communicate their findings.

Jupyter Notebooks are widely used in academia, industry, and research for data exploration, prototyping, and collaboration. Their flexibility, interactivity, and ease of sharing make them a popular choice for data scientists and analysts working on data-driven projects.

Conclusion

Data science tools and libraries are essential for performing various tasks in data analysis, machine learning, and visualization. Python and R are widely used programming languages for data science, with extensive ecosystems of libraries for data manipulation, analysis, and visualization. SQL is essential for querying and analyzing structured data in relational databases. Tableau and Jupyter Notebooks are powerful tools for creating interactive visualizations and conducting exploratory data analysis. By leveraging these tools and libraries, data scientists and analysts can unlock insights from their data and make informed decisions to drive business success.

8. Data Science Methodologies

Data science methodologies are systematic approaches to solving complex problems using data. These methodologies provide a framework for conducting data-driven analyses and deriving actionable insights from data. In this section, we will explore some of the most widely used data science methodologies and their key components.

1. CRISP-DM (Cross-Industry Standard Process for Data Mining)

CRISP-DM is a widely used data mining process model that provides a structured approach to data mining projects. It consists of six phases:

1.1 Business Understanding: In this phase, the goals and objectives of the data mining project are defined. Stakeholders' requirements are gathered, and the problem to be solved is clearly articulated.

1.2 Data Understanding: In this phase, data sources are identified, and data is collected, explored, and assessed for quality and relevance. Data preprocessing steps such as cleaning, transformation, and feature engineering are performed.

1.3 Data Preparation: In this phase, the dataset is prepared for modeling by selecting relevant features, splitting the data into training and testing sets, and performing additional preprocessing steps such as normalization or scaling.

1.4 Modeling: In this phase, machine learning models are selected, trained, and evaluated using the prepared dataset. Different algorithms and techniques are explored to find the best-performing model for the given problem.

1.5 Evaluation: In this phase, the performance of the trained models is evaluated using appropriate metrics and techniques. Models are compared, and the best-performing model is selected for deployment.

1.6 Deployment: In this phase, the selected model is deployed into production, and the results are integrated into business processes. Monitoring and maintenance procedures are established to ensure the continued performance of the deployed model.

CRISP-DM provides a flexible and iterative framework for data mining projects, allowing data scientists to adapt to changing requirements and refine their analyses as needed.

2. KDD (Knowledge Discovery in Databases)

KDD is a process for extracting useful knowledge from large volumes of data. It consists of several stages:

2.1 Selection: In this stage, data is selected from various sources based on its relevance to the problem at hand. Data selection criteria may include data quality, availability, and domain expertise.

2.2 Preprocessing: In this stage, data is cleaned, transformed, and prepared for analysis. Preprocessing steps may include data cleaning, normalization, feature selection, and dimensionality reduction.

2.3 Transformation: In this stage, data is transformed into a format suitable for analysis. This may involve converting categorical variables into numerical ones, scaling data to a common range, or encoding text data into a numerical format.

2.4 Data Mining: In this stage, patterns, trends, and relationships are identified in the data using data mining techniques such as clustering, classification, regression, and association rule mining.

2.5 Interpretation/Evaluation: In this stage, the results of the data mining process are interpreted and evaluated for their relevance and usefulness. This may involve visualizing the results, conducting statistical analyses, and assessing the performance of predictive models.

2.6 Action: In this stage, the knowledge gained from the data mining process is used to make informed decisions and take action. This may involve implementing changes to business processes, developing new products or services, or refining existing strategies.

KDD provides a systematic approach to knowledge discovery from data, enabling organizations to extract valuable insights and make data-driven decisions.

3. Agile Data Science

Agile Data Science is an iterative and collaborative approach to data science projects. It combines principles from agile software development with data science methodologies to deliver value quickly and adapt to changing requirements. Some key principles of Agile Data Science include:

3.1 Iterative Development: Agile Data Science projects are broken down into small, manageable iterations called sprints. Each sprint focuses on delivering a specific set of features or analyses within a fixed time frame, typically two to four weeks.

3.2 Collaboration: Agile Data Science emphasizes collaboration and communication between cross-functional teams, including data scientists, engineers, domain experts, and stakeholders. Regular meetings, such as daily stand-ups and sprint retrospectives, help ensure alignment and transparency throughout the project.

3.3 Continuous Delivery: Agile Data Science promotes continuous delivery of value by prioritizing and delivering high-impact analyses and insights early and often. This allows organizations to validate assumptions, gather feedback, and make course corrections quickly.

3.4 Flexibility: Agile Data Science embraces change and welcomes feedback from stakeholders throughout the project. This flexibility enables teams to respond to new insights, shifting priorities, and emerging requirements effectively.

Agile Data Science enables organizations to rapidly experiment with data, iterate on hypotheses, and deliver actionable insights that drive business value.

4. Lean Data Science

Lean Data Science is a methodology that focuses on maximizing value while minimizing waste in data science projects. It emphasizes efficiency, simplicity, and continuous improvement. Some key principles of Lean Data Science include:

4.1 Value Stream Mapping: Lean Data Science begins with value stream mapping, where the end-to-end process of data science projects is analyzed to identify inefficiencies and opportunities for improvement.

4.2 MVP (Minimum Viable Product): Lean Data Science emphasizes the development of minimum viable products (MVPs) – simple prototypes or analyses that deliver value to stakeholders quickly and with minimal effort.

4.3 Kaizen (Continuous Improvement): Lean Data Science promotes a culture of continuous improvement, where teams regularly reflect on their processes, experiment with new techniques, and implement changes to increase efficiency and effectiveness.

4.4 Waste Reduction: Lean Data Science seeks to eliminate waste in data science projects by focusing on high-value activities, reducing rework, and optimizing resource utilization.

Lean Data Science enables organizations to streamline their data science processes, deliver value more efficiently, and achieve better outcomes with fewer resources.

Conclusion

Data science methodologies provide structured approaches to solving complex problems using data. Whether it's the systematic approach of CRISP-DM, the knowledge discovery process of KDD, the iterative and collaborative approach of Agile Data Science, or the efficiency-focused approach of Lean Data Science, these methodologies offer frameworks for conducting data-driven analyses and deriving actionable insights from data. By leveraging these methodologies, organizations can effectively harness the power of data to drive innovation, optimize processes, and make informed decisions that lead to business success.

9. Ethical Considerations in Data Science

Ethical considerations in data science are essential to ensure that data-driven decisions are made responsibly and ethically. As data science continues to evolve and become more integrated into various aspects of society, it is crucial to address ethical concerns surrounding data privacy, fairness, transparency, and accountability. In this section, we will explore some of the key ethical considerations in data science and their implications.

1. Data Privacy

Data privacy refers to the protection of individuals' personal information and the responsible handling of sensitive data. It is essential to respect individuals' privacy rights and ensure that data is collected, stored, and used in accordance with relevant regulations and best practices. Some key considerations for data privacy include:

1.1 Informed Consent: Organizations should obtain informed consent from individuals before collecting their personal data. This includes providing clear and transparent information about how the data will be used, who will have access to it, and how it will be protected.

1.2 Data Minimization: Organizations should only collect and retain the minimum amount of data necessary for their intended purposes. This helps reduce the risk of unauthorized access, misuse, and data breaches.

1.3 Anonymization and De-identification: Organizations should take measures to anonymize or de-identify personal data to protect individuals' privacy. This may involve removing or encrypting personally identifiable information (PII) from datasets to prevent re-identification.

1.4 Data Security: Organizations should implement robust security measures to protect data from unauthorized access, disclosure, alteration, or destruction. This includes encryption, access controls, data backups, and regular security audits.

Ensuring data privacy is critical to building trust with individuals and maintaining compliance with data protection regulations such as GDPR (General Data Protection Regulation) and CCPA (California Consumer Privacy Act).

2. Fairness and Bias

Fairness and bias refer to the impartiality and equity of algorithms and decision-making processes. It is essential to ensure that data-driven systems do not discriminate against individuals or groups based on protected characteristics such as race, gender, ethnicity, religion, or sexual orientation. Some key considerations for fairness and bias include:

2.1 Bias Detection: Organizations should proactively identify and mitigate biases in data and algorithms to ensure fair and equitable outcomes. This may involve analyzing datasets for biases, testing algorithms for fairness, and implementing bias mitigation techniques.

2.2 Algorithmic Transparency: Organizations should strive to make their algorithms transparent and explainable to users and stakeholders. This includes documenting the data sources, features, and methodologies used in algorithmic decision-making and providing explanations for decisions when requested.

2.3 Diversity and Representation: Organizations should prioritize diversity and representation in their data science teams to ensure diverse perspectives and experiences are considered in the development and deployment of data-driven systems. This can help mitigate biases and promote fairness in decision-making.

2.4 Fairness Metrics: Organizations should develop and use fairness metrics to evaluate the performance of algorithms and decision-making processes across different demographic groups. This helps identify disparities and biases and guide efforts to improve fairness and equity.

Addressing fairness and bias in data science requires ongoing vigilance, collaboration, and commitment to equity and social justice.

3. Transparency and Accountability

Transparency and accountability are essential principles for building trust and ensuring responsible data practices. Organizations should be transparent about their data collection and use practices and be accountable for the consequences of their decisions. Some key considerations for transparency and accountability include:

3.1 Data Governance: Organizations should establish robust data governance frameworks to ensure accountability and compliance with data protection regulations. This includes defining roles and responsibilities, implementing data policies and procedures, and conducting regular audits and assessments.

3.2 Model Transparency: Organizations should strive to make their models transparent and explainable to users and stakeholders. This includes documenting model architectures, parameters, and assumptions and providing explanations for model predictions and recommendations.

3.3 Ethical Guidelines: Organizations should develop and adhere to ethical guidelines and codes of conduct for data science practitioners. This includes promoting ethical behavior, fostering a culture of integrity and accountability, and providing training and resources to support ethical decision-making.

3.4 Stakeholder Engagement: Organizations should engage with stakeholders, including individuals, communities, and advocacy groups, to solicit feedback, address concerns, and promote transparency and accountability in data practices. This helps build trust and foster collaboration in data-driven initiatives.

Transparency and accountability are essential for fostering trust, promoting responsible data practices, and mitigating risks associated with data misuse and abuse.

4. Social Impact

Data science has the potential to have significant social impact, both positive and negative. It is essential to consider the broader societal implications of data-driven technologies and ensure that they benefit individuals and communities equitably. Some key considerations for social impact include:

4.1 Ethical Use Cases: Organizations should prioritize ethical use cases for data science projects that promote social good, such as healthcare, education, environmental conservation, and social justice. This includes addressing societal challenges and advancing the public interest through data-driven innovations.

4.2 Community Engagement: Organizations should engage with communities affected by data-driven technologies to understand their needs, concerns, and preferences. This includes involving community members in the design, development, and evaluation of data-driven systems to ensure they meet local needs and values.

4.3 Equity and Inclusion: Organizations should strive to promote equity and inclusion in data science initiatives by addressing disparities and inequities in access to data, technology, and opportunities. This includes advocating for policies and practices that promote diversity, equity, and inclusion in the data science field.

4.4 Ethical Decision-Making: Organizations should empower data science practitioners to make ethical decisions and prioritize social impact in their work. This includes providing training, resources, and support to help practitioners navigate ethical dilemmas and uphold ethical standards in their work.

By considering the social impact of data science initiatives and prioritizing ethical considerations, organizations can harness the power of data for positive social change and contribute to a more just and equitable society.

Conclusion

Ethical considerations in data science are essential for ensuring that data-driven decisions are made responsibly and ethically. By addressing issues such as data privacy, fairness and bias, transparency and accountability, and social impact, organizations can build trust, promote equity, and foster positive social change through data-driven technologies. By incorporating ethical principles into their data practices, organizations can mitigate risks, maximize benefits, and promote the responsible use of data for the greater good.

10. Data Science Challenges and Limitations

Data science, while immensely powerful, is not without its challenges and limitations. In this section, we will explore some of the key challenges and limitations faced by data scientists and organizations working with data-driven technologies.

1. Data Quality and Quantity

1.1 Data Quality: Ensuring the quality of data is one of the most significant challenges in data science. Poor data quality, such as missing values, inconsistencies, and inaccuracies, can significantly impact the results of data analysis and modeling.

1.2 Data Quantity: While the abundance of data is often seen as a benefit, too much data can also pose challenges. Managing large volumes of data, known as "big data," requires specialized tools and techniques for storage, processing, and analysis.

2. Data Privacy and Security

2.1 Data Privacy: Protecting individuals' privacy and sensitive information is a critical concern in data science. Organizations must comply with data protection regulations and implement robust security measures to prevent unauthorized access, misuse, and breaches of personal data.

2.2 Data Security: Ensuring the security of data is essential to protect against data breaches, cyberattacks, and other security threats. Organizations must implement encryption, access controls, and other security measures to safeguard data from unauthorized access and manipulation.

3. Bias and Fairness

3.1 Bias in Data: Bias in data, such as sampling bias or algorithmic bias, can lead to unfair or discriminatory outcomes. Identifying and mitigating bias in data and algorithms is essential to ensure fairness and equity in data-driven decision-making.

3.2 Fairness in Algorithms: Ensuring fairness in algorithms and decision-making processes is a challenging task. Algorithmic fairness metrics and techniques can help identify and address biases in algorithms, but achieving fairness in practice remains a complex and ongoing effort.

4. Interpretability and Explainability

4.1 Model Interpretability: Understanding how machine learning models make predictions is crucial for building trust and accountability. However, many complex machine learning models, such as deep neural networks, lack interpretability, making it challenging to explain their decisions.

4.2 Explainable AI: Explainable AI techniques aim to make machine learning models more interpretable by providing explanations for their predictions. While these techniques show promise, achieving high levels of interpretability without sacrificing performance remains a significant challenge.

5. Scalability and Performance

5.1 Scalability: Scaling data science projects to handle large volumes of data or increasing computational demands can be challenging. Organizations must invest in scalable infrastructure, such as cloud computing platforms or distributed computing systems, to support growing data needs.

5.2 Performance: Achieving high performance in data analysis and modeling requires efficient algorithms, optimized code, and parallel processing techniques. Tuning algorithms and optimizing code for performance can be time-consuming and resource-intensive.

6. Talent Shortage and Skills Gap

6.1 Talent Shortage: There is a growing demand for skilled data scientists and data analysts, but a shortage of qualified talent to fill these roles. Recruiting and retaining top talent in the field of data science can be challenging for organizations.

6.2 Skills Gap: The field of data science is rapidly evolving, with new tools, techniques, and technologies emerging regularly. Keeping up with the latest developments and acquiring new skills can be challenging for data science professionals, leading to a skills gap in the industry.

7. Ethical and Legal Concerns

7.1 Ethical Concerns: Ethical considerations, such as privacy, fairness, transparency, and accountability, are essential in data science. However, navigating ethical dilemmas and ensuring ethical practices can be challenging, especially in complex data-driven projects.

7.2 Legal Compliance: Organizations must comply with various legal and regulatory requirements related to data protection, privacy, and security. Staying compliant with laws such as GDPR, CCPA, HIPAA, and others requires ongoing monitoring and adherence to best practices.

8. Cost and Resource Constraints

8.1 Cost: Data science projects can be costly, requiring investments in infrastructure, tools, talent, and ongoing maintenance. Managing project budgets and ensuring a return on investment (ROI) can be challenging for organizations, especially smaller ones with limited resources.

8.2 Resource Constraints: Limited access to data, computing resources, and expertise can pose significant challenges for organizations embarking on data science projects. Overcoming resource constraints requires creative solutions and strategic planning.

9. Complexity and Interdisciplinary Nature

9.1 Complexity: Data science projects often involve complex data, algorithms, and methodologies that can be challenging to understand and implement. Managing project complexity requires effective communication, collaboration, and project management.

9.2 Interdisciplinary Nature: Data science is an interdisciplinary field that draws on knowledge and skills from various domains, including statistics, computer science, mathematics, and domain expertise. Collaborating across disciplines and integrating diverse perspectives can be challenging but essential for successful data science projects.

10. Cultural and Organizational Challenges

10.1 Cultural Shift: Adopting a data-driven culture and mindset within organizations can be challenging, requiring changes in attitudes, behaviors, and decision-making processes. Overcoming resistance to change and promoting data-driven decision-making requires leadership, communication, and education.

10.2 Organizational Silos: Siloed data and organizational structures can hinder data integration, collaboration, and knowledge sharing within organizations. Breaking down silos and fostering cross-functional collaboration is essential for leveraging data effectively and driving business outcomes.

Conclusion

Data science faces numerous challenges and limitations, ranging from data quality and privacy concerns to bias and fairness in algorithms, interpretability of models, scalability and performance issues, talent shortage and skills gap, ethical and legal concerns, cost and resource constraints, complexity and interdisciplinary nature of the field, and cultural and organizational challenges. Overcoming these challenges requires concerted efforts from data scientists, organizations, policymakers, and society as a whole. By addressing these challenges and limitations, data science can fulfill its potential to drive innovation, solve complex problems, and create positive social impact.

'Data Science' in Modern Technology

The Application of Data Science in Modern Technology

Data science has emerged as a transformative force in modern technology, revolutionizing industries and driving innovation across various sectors. Its application spans from business intelligence and healthcare to finance, manufacturing, and beyond. Let's delve into the intricate ways data science is applied in modern technology:

1. Predictive Analytics

Predictive analytics is one of the primary applications of data science. By leveraging historical data and advanced algorithms, organizations can forecast future trends, behaviors, and events. In finance, predictive analytics helps detect fraudulent transactions, optimize investment strategies, and predict market trends. Similarly, in e-commerce, it powers recommendation systems that suggest products to users based on their past behavior and preferences.

2. Machine Learning and Artificial Intelligence

Machine learning (ML) and artificial intelligence (AI) are integral components of data science, enabling systems to learn from data and make intelligent decisions without explicit programming. In healthcare, ML algorithms analyze medical images to assist in disease diagnosis, predict patient outcomes, and personalize treatment plans. In autonomous vehicles, AI algorithms process sensor data to navigate safely and efficiently through traffic.

3. Natural Language Processing (NLP)

NLP is a branch of artificial intelligence that focuses on the interaction between computers and human language. It enables machines to understand, interpret, and generate human language in a meaningful way. NLP powers virtual assistants like Siri, Alexa, and Google Assistant, which respond to voice commands, answer questions, and perform tasks based on natural language input. Additionally, NLP is used in sentiment analysis, chatbots, and language translation.

4. Computer Vision

Computer vision involves teaching computers to interpret and understand the visual world. It encompasses tasks such as image classification, object detection, and facial recognition. In retail, computer vision is used for inventory management, customer tracking, and cashier-less checkout systems. In security, it aids in surveillance, identifying suspicious activities, and monitoring crowd behavior.

5. Personalized Marketing

Data science enables organizations to create personalized marketing campaigns tailored to individual preferences and behaviors. By analyzing customer data, including demographics, browsing history, and purchase patterns, marketers can deliver targeted advertisements, promotions, and recommendations. Personalized marketing increases engagement, conversion rates, and customer satisfaction.

6. Fraud Detection

Fraud detection is a critical application of data science in industries such as banking, insurance, and e-commerce. ML algorithms analyze transaction data to identify fraudulent activities, such as unauthorized transactions, identity theft, and account takeovers. By detecting and preventing fraud in real-time, organizations can minimize financial losses and protect customer assets.

7. Supply Chain Optimization

Data science optimizes supply chain operations by analyzing vast amounts of data related to inventory levels, demand forecasts, transportation routes, and supplier performance. ML algorithms optimize inventory management, streamline logistics, and reduce transportation costs. By optimizing the supply chain, organizations can improve efficiency, reduce waste, and enhance customer satisfaction.

8. Healthcare Analytics

Healthcare analytics leverages data science to improve patient outcomes, streamline operations, and reduce costs in the healthcare industry. ML algorithms analyze electronic health records (EHRs), medical images, and genomic data to assist in disease diagnosis, treatment planning, and patient monitoring. Healthcare analytics also enables population health management, predictive modeling for disease outbreaks, and personalized medicine.

9. Energy Management

Data science plays a crucial role in energy management by optimizing energy production, distribution, and consumption. ML algorithms analyze data from smart meters, sensors, and weather forecasts to predict energy demand, optimize grid operations, and identify energy-saving opportunities. Energy management solutions enable utilities to reduce costs, improve reliability, and integrate renewable energy sources into the grid.

10. Social Media Analysis

Social media analysis involves extracting insights from social media data to understand customer sentiment, identify trends, and inform marketing strategies. NLP algorithms analyze text data from social media platforms to monitor brand mentions, detect emerging issues, and engage with customers. Social media analysis also helps organizations measure the impact of marketing campaigns, identify influencers, and track competitor activities.

Conclusion

The application of data science in modern technology is vast and diverse, encompassing predictive analytics, machine learning, natural language processing, computer vision, personalized marketing, fraud detection, supply chain optimization, healthcare analytics, energy management, and social media analysis, among others. By harnessing the power of data science, organizations can gain valuable insights, drive innovation, and make data-driven decisions that lead to business success and societal impact. As technology continues to evolve, data science will remain at the forefront, shaping the future of industries and transforming the way we live, work, and interact with the world.

Application of 'Data Science' in Modern Human Life

The Application of Data Science in Modern Human Life

In the digital age, data science has become deeply intertwined with various aspects of modern human life, influencing how we work, communicate, make decisions, and interact with the world around us. From personalized recommendations on streaming platforms to advanced healthcare diagnostics, data science touches almost every facet of our daily lives. Let's explore some of the prominent applications of data science in modern human life:

1. Personalized Recommendations

Data science powers personalized recommendations on e-commerce websites, streaming platforms, and social media platforms. By analyzing user behavior, preferences, and interactions, algorithms suggest products, movies, music, and content tailored to individual tastes. These recommendations enhance user experience, increase engagement, and drive sales.

2. Healthcare Diagnostics

In healthcare, data science plays a crucial role in diagnostics, treatment planning, and patient care. Machine learning algorithms analyze medical images, electronic health records (EHRs), and genomic data to assist in disease diagnosis, predict patient outcomes, and personalize treatment plans. Data-driven insights improve healthcare outcomes, reduce medical errors, and enhance patient safety.

3. Smart Home Technology

Data science powers smart home technology, enabling devices to learn and adapt to users' preferences and behaviors. Smart thermostats adjust temperature settings based on occupancy and weather forecasts, while smart lighting systems adjust brightness and color temperature to create the desired ambiance. These technologies enhance comfort, convenience, and energy efficiency in the home.

4. Traffic Management

Data science optimizes traffic management systems by analyzing traffic patterns, congestion, and vehicle flow. ML algorithms predict traffic conditions, recommend optimal routes, and control traffic signals to reduce congestion and improve traffic flow. Real-time traffic data and navigation apps help drivers avoid delays and reach their destinations more efficiently.

5. Financial Services

In the financial services industry, data science drives risk assessment, fraud detection, and investment strategies.

ML algorithms analyze transaction data to detect fraudulent activities, predict creditworthiness, and identify investment opportunities. Automated trading algorithms execute trades based on market trends and predictive analytics, optimizing portfolio performance.

6. Personal Finance Management

Data science enables individuals to manage their personal finances more effectively. Personal finance apps analyze income, expenses, and savings patterns to provide insights into spending habits, budgeting, and goal setting. ML algorithms offer personalized financial advice, recommend savings strategies, and help users track progress towards financial goals.

7. Social Media and Networking

Data science fuels social media platforms and networking sites, facilitating connections, content discovery, and engagement. NLP algorithms analyze text data to understand user sentiment, detect trends, and recommend relevant content. Social media analytics tools provide insights into audience demographics, engagement metrics, and content performance, helping users and businesses optimize their social media presence.

8. Education and Learning

In education, data science enhances teaching and learning experiences through personalized learning platforms, adaptive assessments, and educational analytics. ML algorithms analyze student performance data to identify learning gaps, provide targeted interventions, and personalize learning pathways. Data-driven insights empower educators to tailor instruction to individual student needs and improve learning outcomes.

9. Urban Planning and Development

Data science informs urban planning and development initiatives by analyzing demographic trends, transportation patterns, and infrastructure usage. GIS (Geographic Information System) technologies visualize spatial data, identify areas of congestion or underutilization, and inform city planning decisions. Data-driven insights support sustainable urban development, improve public services, and enhance quality of life for residents.

10. Environmental Monitoring and Conservation

Data science contributes to environmental monitoring and conservation efforts by analyzing environmental data, satellite imagery, and sensor data. ML algorithms predict environmental phenomena such as climate change, deforestation, and wildlife habitat loss. Data-driven insights inform conservation strategies, habitat restoration efforts, and climate adaptation initiatives, promoting environmental sustainability and biodiversity conservation.

Conclusion

The application of data science in modern human life is diverse and far-reaching, impacting how we shop, learn, travel, communicate, and live. From personalized recommendations and healthcare diagnostics to smart home technology and environmental conservation, data science enhances our daily experiences, drives innovation, and addresses societal challenges. As technology continues to evolve, data science will play an increasingly vital role in shaping the future of human life and society, empowering individuals, businesses, and communities to thrive in a data-driven world.

Application of 'Data Science' in Modern Cybersecurity

The Application of Data Science in Modern Cybersecurity

In an increasingly interconnected world, cybersecurity has become a critical concern for individuals, businesses, and governments alike. With the proliferation of cyber threats and attacks, organizations are turning to data science to bolster their cybersecurity defenses. Data science offers advanced analytical techniques and machine learning algorithms that can detect, prevent, and mitigate cyber threats more effectively than traditional methods. Let's explore the elaborate application of data science in modern cybersecurity:

1. Threat Detection and Prevention

Data science enables organizations to detect and prevent cyber threats in real-time by analyzing vast amounts of data for anomalous patterns and indicators of compromise. Machine learning algorithms, such as anomaly detection, clustering, and classification, identify suspicious activities, unauthorized access attempts, and malware infections. By analyzing network traffic, system logs, and user behavior, data science models can proactively identify potential threats before they cause harm.

2. Intrusion Detection Systems (IDS)

Intrusion detection systems (IDS) leverage data science techniques to monitor networks and systems for signs of malicious activity or unauthorized access. ML algorithms analyze network traffic, system logs, and security events to detect anomalous behavior, known attack patterns, and signatures of malware. IDS solutions can alert security teams to potential security breaches, enabling them to respond quickly and mitigate the impact of cyber attacks.

3. Malware Analysis and Classification

Data science plays a crucial role in malware analysis and classification, helping security researchers identify and classify malicious software based on its characteristics and behavior. ML algorithms analyze file attributes, code structures, and runtime behavior to classify malware into different categories, such as viruses, worms, trojans, and ransomware. By understanding the characteristics of malware, cybersecurity professionals can develop more effective countermeasures and mitigation strategies.

4. User and Entity Behavior Analytics (UEBA)

User and entity behavior analytics (UEBA) solutions use data science to analyze user behavior and detect insider threats, compromised accounts, and abnormal activities. ML algorithms model normal user behavior based on historical data and identify deviations from normal patterns that may indicate security incidents. UEBA solutions can detect insider threats, such as data exfiltration, privilege escalation, and unauthorized access, by monitoring user activities across multiple systems and applications.

5. Fraud Detection and Prevention

Data science is widely used in fraud detection and prevention systems to identify fraudulent transactions, account takeovers, and fraudulent activities. ML algorithms analyze transaction data, user behavior, and historical patterns to detect anomalies and identify suspicious activities indicative of fraud. By leveraging advanced analytics and machine learning techniques, organizations can detect fraud in real-time, reduce false positives, and mitigate financial losses.

6. Security Information and Event Management (SIEM)

Security information and event management (SIEM) systems collect, correlate, and analyze security events and log data from various sources to detect and respond to security incidents. Data science techniques, such as correlation analysis, pattern recognition, and predictive modeling, enable SIEM solutions to identify security threats, prioritize alerts, and automate incident response workflows. By aggregating and analyzing security data in real-time, SIEM solutions help organizations detect and respond to cyber threats more effectively.

7. Vulnerability Assessment and Patch Management

Data science is used in vulnerability assessment and patch management processes to identify security vulnerabilities in software and systems and prioritize remediation efforts. ML algorithms analyze vulnerability data, exploit patterns, and threat intelligence feeds to assess the likelihood and impact of potential security vulnerabilities. By prioritizing vulnerabilities based on risk factors and exploitability, organizations can allocate resources more effectively and reduce the likelihood of successful cyber attacks.

8. Security Analytics and Threat Intelligence

Security analytics and threat intelligence platforms leverage data science techniques to analyze security data, threat feeds, and intelligence sources to identify emerging threats and cyber attack trends. ML algorithms analyze historical data, malware samples, and security events to identify patterns, correlations, and indicators of compromise. By providing actionable insights and context-rich intelligence, security analytics platforms empower security teams to make informed decisions and respond to cyber threats more effectively.

Conclusion

Data science has become indispensable in modern cybersecurity, providing advanced analytical techniques and machine learning algorithms that enable organizations to detect, prevent, and mitigate cyber threats more effectively. From threat detection and intrusion detection to malware analysis and fraud detection, data science plays a crucial role in safeguarding organizations' digital assets and protecting against cyber attacks. As cyber threats continue to evolve and become more sophisticated, the application of data science in cybersecurity will remain essential for ensuring the security and resilience of digital systems and infrastructure.

What is the 'Data Analysis'?

Data Analysis is the process of inspecting, cleaning, transforming, and interpreting data with the goal of extracting useful information, informing conclusions, and supporting decision-making. It involves applying various statistical, mathematical, and computational techniques to analyze datasets and uncover patterns, trends, correlations, and insights that can inform business strategies, scientific research, policy decisions, and more.

The key steps involved in data analysis include:

1. **Data Collection:** Gathering relevant data from various sources, including databases, files, surveys, sensors, and web sources.
2. **Data Cleaning:** Preprocessing the data to handle missing values, outliers, errors, and inconsistencies, ensuring data quality and integrity.
3. **Exploratory Data Analysis (EDA):** Exploring the dataset visually and statistically to understand its structure, distribution, and relationships between variables.
4. **Data Transformation:** Transforming the data through techniques such as normalization, standardization, aggregation, and feature engineering to prepare it for analysis.
5. **Statistical Analysis:** Applying statistical techniques, such as hypothesis testing, regression analysis, and clustering, to identify patterns, trends, and relationships in the data.
6. **Machine Learning:** Employing machine learning algorithms, such as classification, regression, clustering, and anomaly detection, to build predictive models and uncover insights from the data.
7. **Data Visualization:** Visualizing the results of the analysis using charts, graphs, and dashboards to

communicate findings effectively and facilitate
decision-making.

8. **Interpretation and Reporting:** Interpreting the
   results of the analysis in the context of the
   problem domain and communicating findings to
   stakeholders through reports, presentations, and
   recommendations.

Data analysis is used across various domains and
industries, including business, finance, healthcare,
marketing, science, engineering, and social sciences, to
gain insights, solve complex problems, optimize
processes, and drive innovation. It plays a crucial role in
transforming raw data into actionable intelligence,
enabling organizations and individuals to make informed
decisions and achieve their objectives.

What is the difference between 'Data Science and Data Analysis'?

Data Science and **Data Analysis** are closely related
fields that involve working with data to extract insights
and make informed decisions. While they share some
similarities, they also have distinct differences in terms
of scope, methods, and objectives.

1. Scope:

- **Data Science:** Data science encompasses a
  broader range of activities, including data
  collection, data cleaning, data preprocessing,
  machine learning, statistical modeling, and
  deployment of predictive models. It involves not
  only analyzing data but also extracting
  knowledge and insights, building predictive

models, and creating data-driven solutions to complex problems.

- **Data Analysis:** Data analysis focuses primarily on inspecting, cleaning, transforming, and interpreting data to extract useful information and inform decision-making. It involves applying statistical and computational techniques to analyze datasets and uncover patterns, trends, and correlations.

2. Methods:

- **Data Science:** Data science employs a wide range of techniques and methodologies, including machine learning, deep learning, natural language processing, computer vision, and big data analytics. Data scientists often use programming languages such as Python, R, and SQL, as well as tools and libraries like TensorFlow, scikit-learn, and PyTorch.
- **Data Analysis:** Data analysis primarily involves statistical methods, exploratory data analysis (EDA), hypothesis testing, regression analysis, and data visualization techniques. Analysts use tools like Excel, R, Python, and SQL to clean, explore, and analyze data.

3. Objectives:

- **Data Science:** The primary objective of data science is to extract actionable insights from data, build predictive models, and develop data-driven solutions to address complex problems. Data scientists focus on predicting future outcomes, optimizing processes, and uncovering hidden patterns in data to drive business value and innovation.

- **Data Analysis:** The primary objective of data analysis is to understand and interpret data to answer specific questions, solve particular problems, or support decision-making. Data analysts focus on descriptive and diagnostic analysis to identify trends, correlations, and insights that can inform strategies and actions.

4. Skill Sets:

- **Data Science:** Data scientists typically possess a combination of skills in programming, statistics, machine learning, data visualization, and domain expertise. They are proficient in programming languages like Python or R, and they have a deep understanding of algorithms and statistical techniques.
- **Data Analysis:** Data analysts are skilled in data manipulation, data visualization, statistical analysis, and problem-solving. They have strong analytical skills, attention to detail, and the ability to interpret complex data sets effectively.

Conclusion:

While data science and data analysis share common goals of extracting insights from data, they differ in scope, methods, objectives, and skill sets. Data science encompasses a broader range of activities, including machine learning and predictive modeling, while data analysis focuses primarily on exploring and interpreting data using statistical techniques. Both fields play essential roles in leveraging data to drive informed decision-making and achieve business objectives.

100 Questions and Answer about 'Data Science'

Questions About Data Science:

1. What is data science?
2. What are the key components of data science?
3. How is data science different from traditional statistics?
4. What are some common applications of data science?
5. What role does data cleaning play in data science?
6. What is the importance of exploratory data analysis (EDA) in data science?
7. How do machine learning algorithms contribute to data science?
8. What is the significance of feature engineering in machine learning?
9. What are some popular programming languages used in data science?
10. How does data visualization enhance data analysis in data science?
11. What are some challenges faced in the field of data science?
12. How do data scientists handle big data?
13. What is predictive modeling, and how is it used in data science?
14. What are some ethical considerations in data science?
15. How does data science contribute to business intelligence?
16. What are the steps involved in a typical data science project?
17. What is the role of statistics in data science?

18. How do data scientists evaluate the performance of machine learning models?
19. What are some techniques used for anomaly detection in data science?
20. How is natural language processing (NLP) applied in data science?
21. What is the difference between supervised and unsupervised learning?
22. How do data scientists address bias in machine learning models?
23. What is reinforcement learning, and how is it used in data science?
24. What are some common clustering algorithms used in data science?
25. How do data scientists handle missing data in datasets?
26. What is time series analysis, and when is it used in data science?
27. What role does data engineering play in the data science process?
28. How do data scientists ensure the security and privacy of data?
29. What are some real-world examples of successful data science projects?
30. How does data science contribute to personalized medicine?
31. What is the difference between classification and regression in machine learning?
32. How do data scientists select the most appropriate machine learning algorithm for a given task?
33. What is cross-validation, and why is it important in machine learning?
34. What is the role of feature selection in machine learning?

35. How do data scientists handle imbalanced datasets?
36. What is ensemble learning, and how is it used in machine learning?
37. How do data scientists deploy machine learning models into production?
38. What are some common performance metrics used in evaluating machine learning models?
39. How does data science contribute to fraud detection in finance?
40. What role does sentiment analysis play in social media analytics?
41. How does data science contribute to customer segmentation and targeting in marketing?
42. What is deep learning, and how is it different from traditional machine learning?
43. How do data scientists interpret the results of a machine learning model?
44. What is the bias-variance tradeoff, and how does it affect machine learning models?
45. How do data scientists assess the reliability and validity of data sources?
46. What are some common feature extraction techniques used in data science?
47. How does dimensionality reduction improve the performance of machine learning models?
48. What are some challenges associated with working with unstructured data in data science?
49. How do data scientists handle overfitting in machine learning models?
50. What is the role of regularization in preventing overfitting in machine learning?
51. How does data science contribute to supply chain optimization?
52. What is A/B testing, and how is it used in data science?

53. How do data scientists measure the impact of their models on business outcomes?
54. What are some common data visualization techniques used in data science?
55. How does data science contribute to risk assessment in insurance?
56. What is the role of recommendation systems in e-commerce?
57. How do data scientists address multicollinearity in regression analysis?
58. What is the difference between batch processing and real-time processing in data science?
59. How do data scientists handle skewed distributions in datasets?
60. What is the role of data science in environmental monitoring and conservation?
61. How does data science contribute to weather forecasting and climate modeling?
62. What is the impact of data science on cybersecurity?
63. How do data scientists handle time series data in forecasting models?
64. What are some common data preprocessing techniques used in data science?
65. How does data science contribute to optimizing marketing campaigns?
66. What is the role of optimization algorithms in data science?
67. How do data scientists identify outliers in datasets?
68. What is the difference between batch learning and online learning in machine learning?
69. How does data science contribute to improving operational efficiency in manufacturing?
70. What are some common data storage and retrieval techniques used in data science?

71. How do data scientists address multicollinearity in regression analysis?
72. What is the role of data science in improving educational outcomes?
73. How does data science contribute to urban planning and development?
74. What are some common data integration techniques used in data science?
75. How do data scientists handle data imbalance in classification tasks?
76. What is the role of data science in optimizing energy consumption and conservation?
77. How does data science contribute to optimizing healthcare delivery and patient outcomes?
78. What are some common challenges associated with deploying machine learning models into production?
79. How do data scientists address model interpretability and explainability?
80. What is the role of data science in optimizing inventory management and supply chain logistics?
81. How do data scientists handle nonlinear relationships in regression analysis?
82. What are some common techniques used for time series forecasting in data science?
83. How does data science contribute to improving customer experience in retail?
84. What is the role of data science in improving transportation systems and traffic management?
85. How do data scientists handle bias and fairness issues in machine learning models?
86. What is the difference between structured and unstructured data in data science?
87. How does data science contribute to personalized recommendations in online platforms?

88. What are some common data preprocessing techniques used for text data?
89. How do data scientists handle data drift and concept drift in machine learning models?
90. What is the role of data science in optimizing pricing strategies and revenue management?
91. How do data scientists address the curse of dimensionality in machine learning?
92. What are some common techniques used for feature scaling in data science?
93. How does data science contribute to optimizing agricultural practices and crop yield prediction?
94. What is the role of data science in optimizing customer churn prediction and retention strategies?
95. How do data scientists address the cold start problem in recommendation systems?
96. What are some common techniques used for data imputation in data science?
97. How does data science contribute to improving disaster response and emergency management?
98. What is the role of data science in optimizing inventory forecasting and demand planning?
99. How do data scientists handle interpretability and transparency in complex machine learning models?
100.   What are some emerging trends and future directions in the field of data science?

Answers Of Above Questions:

1. Data science is an interdisciplinary field that involves extracting insights and knowledge from structured and unstructured data using various techniques and methodologies.

2. The key components of data science include data collection, data cleaning, exploratory data analysis, machine learning, data visualization, and deployment of predictive models.
3. Data science differs from traditional statistics in its focus on predictive modeling, machine learning, and the use of large-scale datasets.
4. Common applications of data science include predictive analytics, machine learning, natural language processing, computer vision, and big data analytics.
5. Data cleaning is the process of identifying and correcting errors, inconsistencies, and missing values in datasets to ensure data quality and integrity.
6. Exploratory data analysis (EDA) involves visualizing and summarizing data to understand its structure, distribution, and relationships between variables.
7. Machine learning algorithms contribute to data science by enabling systems to learn from data, make predictions, and uncover patterns without being explicitly programmed.
8. Feature engineering involves selecting, transforming, and creating new features from raw data to improve the performance of machine learning models.
9. Popular programming languages used in data science include Python, R, and SQL, along with libraries and frameworks like TensorFlow, scikit-learn, and PyTorch.
10. Data visualization enhances data analysis by providing visual representations of data that

facilitate understanding, interpretation, and communication of insights.

11. Some challenges faced in the field of data science include handling big data, ensuring data privacy and security, addressing bias in algorithms, and dealing with the interpretability of complex models.

12. Data scientists handle big data by using distributed computing frameworks like Apache Hadoop and Apache Spark, as well as storage solutions like Hadoop Distributed File System (HDFS) and NoSQL databases.

13. Predictive modeling involves using historical data to make predictions about future outcomes, such as customer behavior, sales trends, or stock prices.

14. Ethical considerations in data science include ensuring data privacy and security, preventing bias in algorithms, and maintaining transparency and accountability in decision-making processes.

15. Data science contributes to business intelligence by providing insights and actionable recommendations based on data analysis, helping organizations make informed decisions and optimize their operations.

16. The steps involved in a typical data science project include defining the problem, collecting and cleaning data, exploring and analyzing the data, building and evaluating predictive models, and deploying the models into production.

17. Statistics play a crucial role in data science by providing techniques for analyzing data, making inferences, and testing hypotheses.

18. Data scientists evaluate the performance of machine learning models using metrics such as accuracy, precision, recall, F1 score, and area under the ROC curve (AUC).
19. Anomaly detection techniques in data science include statistical methods, machine learning algorithms like isolation forests and one-class SVM, and unsupervised learning approaches.
20. Natural language processing (NLP) is applied in data science to analyze and understand human language, enabling tasks such as sentiment analysis, text classification, and language translation.
21. Supervised learning involves training a model on labeled data, where the input-output pairs are provided, while unsupervised learning involves training a model on unlabeled data, where the model learns patterns and structures from the input data without explicit supervision.
22. Data scientists address bias in machine learning models by carefully selecting training data, using fair and unbiased algorithms, and implementing techniques like bias mitigation and fairness-aware learning.
23. Reinforcement learning is a type of machine learning where an agent learns to make decisions by interacting with an environment and receiving feedback in the form of rewards or penalties.
24. Common clustering algorithms used in data science include K-means clustering, hierarchical clustering, and DBSCAN (Density-Based Spatial Clustering of Applications with Noise).

25. Data scientists handle missing data in datasets by imputing missing values, removing incomplete records, or using techniques like mean imputation, median imputation, or predictive modeling.
26. Time series analysis involves analyzing and forecasting data points collected over time, such as stock prices, weather data, or sensor readings.
27. Data engineering involves designing, building, and maintaining systems for collecting, storing, and processing data, as well as ensuring data quality, reliability, and scalability.
28. Data scientists ensure the security and privacy of data by implementing encryption, access controls, and data anonymization techniques, as well as complying with regulations like GDPR and HIPAA.
29. Real-world examples of successful data science projects include recommendation systems like those used by Netflix and Amazon, predictive maintenance systems in manufacturing, and fraud detection systems in finance.
30. Data science contributes to personalized medicine by analyzing genomic data, electronic health records, and medical imaging to tailor treatments and interventions to individual patients.
31. Classification involves categorizing data into predefined classes or categories, while regression involves predicting continuous values based on input features.
32. Data scientists select the most appropriate machine learning algorithm for a given task

based on factors such as the nature of the data, the problem domain, the available computational resources, and the desired performance metrics.

33. Cross-validation is a technique used to evaluate the performance of machine learning models by splitting the dataset into multiple subsets, training the model on some subsets, and testing it on others to assess its generalization ability.

34. Feature selection involves identifying the most relevant features or variables in a dataset and removing irrelevant or redundant ones to improve the performance of machine learning models and reduce overfitting.

35. Data scientists handle imbalanced datasets by using techniques such as resampling (oversampling or undersampling), cost-sensitive learning, and ensemble methods to address the class imbalance and improve model performance.

36. Ensemble learning is a machine learning technique that combines multiple models (e.g., decision trees, neural networks) to improve prediction accuracy, robustness, and generalization ability.

37. Data scientists deploy machine learning models into production by integrating them into existing software systems, implementing APIs for model inference, and monitoring their performance and reliability in real-world environments.

38. Common performance metrics used in evaluating machine learning models include accuracy, precision, recall, F1 score, area under the ROC curve (AUC), and mean

squared error (MSE), depending on the nature of the task.

39. Data science contributes to fraud detection in finance by analyzing transaction data, user behavior, and other relevant factors to detect suspicious activities, unauthorized access attempts, and fraudulent transactions.

40. Sentiment analysis in social media analytics involves analyzing text data from social media platforms to determine the sentiment (positive, negative, neutral) expressed in user-generated content such as tweets, comments, and reviews.

41. Data science contributes to customer segmentation and targeting in marketing by analyzing customer demographics, behavior, and preferences to identify distinct segments and tailor marketing strategies and campaigns to target specific customer groups effectively.

42. Deep learning is a subset of machine learning that involves training neural networks with multiple layers (deep architectures) to learn complex patterns and representations from data, enabling tasks such as image recognition, speech recognition, and natural language processing.

43. Data scientists interpret the results of a machine learning model by analyzing model predictions, feature importance, model coefficients, and other relevant factors to understand how the model makes decisions and provide insights to stakeholders.

44. The bias-variance tradeoff refers to the tradeoff between bias and variance in machine learning models, where increasing model complexity reduces bias but increases

variance, and vice versa, affecting the model's ability to generalize to unseen data.

45. Data scientists assess the reliability and validity of data sources by evaluating factors such as data accuracy, completeness, consistency, timeliness, and relevance, as well as considering the source's reputation, credibility, and potential biases.

46. Feature extraction techniques in data science involve transforming raw data into a more compact and informative representation by extracting relevant features or characteristics that capture the underlying structure and patterns in the data.

47. Dimensionality reduction techniques such as principal component analysis (PCA) and t-distributed stochastic neighbor embedding (t-SNE) reduce the number of features or dimensions in a dataset while preserving as much information as possible, helping to visualize and analyze high-dimensional data and improve the performance of machine learning models.

48. Challenges associated with working with unstructured data in data science include extracting meaningful information from text, images, and other unstructured formats, dealing with noise and variability, and handling large volumes of data efficiently.

49. Overfitting occurs when a machine learning model learns the training data too well, capturing noise and irrelevant patterns that do not generalize well to unseen data, resulting in poor performance on test data.

50. Regularization techniques such as L1 regularization (Lasso) and L2 regularization

(Ridge) penalize the complexity of a model by adding regularization terms to the loss function, helping to prevent overfitting and improve the model's generalization ability.

51. Data science contributes to supply chain optimization by analyzing supply chain data, identifying inefficiencies, bottlenecks, and risks, and optimizing inventory management, logistics, and distribution processes to reduce costs and improve efficiency.

52. A/B testing is a statistical method used in data science to compare two or more versions of a product, feature, or marketing campaign to determine which one performs better based on predefined metrics such as conversion rate, click-through rate, or revenue.

53. Data scientists measure the impact of their models on business outcomes by tracking key performance indicators (KPIs) and metrics relevant to the specific business objectives, such as revenue, customer retention, cost savings, or user engagement.

54. Data visualization techniques in data science include bar charts, line charts, scatter plots, histograms, heatmaps, and interactive dashboards, which help to visually explore and communicate insights from data effectively.

55. Data science contributes to risk assessment in insurance by analyzing historical claims data, customer demographics, and other relevant factors to assess the likelihood and severity of risks, determine insurance premiums, and develop risk mitigation strategies.

56. Recommendation systems in e-commerce use data science techniques such as collaborative

filtering, content-based filtering, and hybrid approaches to analyze user preferences and behaviors and recommend personalized products or content to users, enhancing the shopping experience and increasing sales.

57. Data scientists address multicollinearity in regression analysis by identifying and removing highly correlated predictor variables, transforming variables, or using regularization techniques to penalize the coefficients of correlated variables, helping to improve model interpretability and stability.

58. Batch processing involves processing data in large, finite batches, while real-time processing involves processing data continuously and immediately as it arrives, enabling faster insights and decision-making in data science applications.

59. Data scientists handle skewed distributions in datasets by applying transformations such as logarithmic transformation, square root transformation, or Box-Cox transformation to make the data more normally distributed and improve the performance of statistical models.

60. Data science contributes to environmental monitoring and conservation by analyzing environmental data such as satellite imagery, sensor data, and biodiversity records to monitor ecosystem health, track environmental changes, and inform conservation efforts and policy decisions.

61. Data science contributes to weather forecasting and climate modeling by analyzing historical weather data, satellite observations, and climate models to predict

future weather patterns, understand climate change trends, and assess potential impacts on ecosystems and human populations.

62. The impact of data science on cybersecurity includes detecting and preventing cyber threats, analyzing security incidents, identifying vulnerabilities, and enhancing incident response capabilities to protect against cyber attacks and ensure the security of digital assets.

63. Data scientists handle time series data in forecasting models by applying techniques such as autoregressive integrated moving average (ARIMA), exponential smoothing (ETS), and machine learning algorithms to capture temporal patterns and make accurate predictions.

64. Common data preprocessing techniques used in data science include data cleaning, data transformation, feature scaling, feature extraction, and dimensionality reduction, which help to prepare raw data for analysis and modeling.

65. Data science contributes to optimizing marketing campaigns by analyzing customer data, segmenting audiences, predicting customer behavior, and optimizing marketing strategies and channels to increase conversions, improve ROI, and enhance customer engagement.

66. Optimization algorithms in data science include techniques such as gradient descent, genetic algorithms, simulated annealing, and particle swarm optimization, which are used to find the optimal solution to complex optimization problems.

67. Data scientists identify outliers in datasets by analyzing data distributions, applying statistical methods such as z-score or interquartile range (IQR), and visualizing data using box plots or scatter plots to detect data points that deviate significantly from the rest.

68. Batch learning involves training a model on a fixed dataset and updating the model periodically with new data, while online learning involves continuously updating the model as new data becomes available, enabling adaptive and incremental learning in data science applications.

69. Data scientists address interpretability and transparency in complex machine learning models by using techniques such as model-agnostic interpretability methods, surrogate models, and explanation methods to explain model predictions and decision-making processes.

70. Data science contributes to optimizing energy consumption and conservation by analyzing energy usage data, identifying inefficiencies, and optimizing energy management systems to reduce energy consumption, lower costs, and minimize environmental impact.

71. Data scientists address the curse of dimensionality in machine learning by applying dimensionality reduction techniques, feature selection methods, and regularization techniques to reduce the number of features or dimensions in high-dimensional datasets, improving model performance and interpretability.

72. Data science contributes to improving educational outcomes by analyzing student

performance data, identifying learning patterns and obstacles, personalizing learning experiences, and developing data-driven interventions to support student success and achievement.

73. Data science contributes to urban planning and development by analyzing demographic data, transportation patterns, land use data, and environmental factors to inform urban planning decisions, optimize infrastructure investments, and improve quality of life for residents.

74. Common data integration techniques used in data science include extract, transform, load (ETL) processes, data virtualization, and data federation, which help to combine and unify data from multiple sources for analysis and decision-making.

75. Data scientists handle data imbalance in classification tasks by using techniques such as resampling methods (oversampling or undersampling), cost-sensitive learning algorithms, and ensemble methods to address class imbalance and improve model performance.

76. Data scientists contribute to improving disaster response and emergency management by analyzing disaster data, predicting disaster risks, optimizing resource allocation, and developing early warning systems to mitigate the impact of disasters and save lives.

77. Data science plays a crucial role in optimizing inventory forecasting and demand planning by analyzing historical sales data, market trends, and supply chain data to predict future demand, optimize inventory

levels, and reduce stockouts and overstock situations.

78. Data scientists address bias and fairness issues in machine learning models by carefully selecting training data, auditing models for bias, and implementing fairness-aware algorithms and techniques to ensure equitable outcomes for all individuals or groups.

79. Structured data refers to data that is organized into a predefined format with a fixed schema, such as databases or spreadsheets, while unstructured data refers to data that does not have a predefined structure or format, such as text documents, images, or audio files.

80. Data science contributes to personalized recommendations in online platforms by analyzing user behavior, preferences, and interactions to generate personalized recommendations for products, services, or content, enhancing user engagement and satisfaction.

81. Data scientists contribute to optimizing healthcare delivery and patient outcomes by analyzing electronic health records, medical imaging data, and genomic data to improve diagnosis, treatment, and patient care, as well as to develop personalized medicine approaches.

82. Data science handles nonlinear relationships in regression analysis by using nonlinear regression models, polynomial regression, spline regression, or kernel methods to capture complex relationships between variables and make accurate predictions.

83. Common techniques used for time series forecasting in data science include autoregressive integrated moving average (ARIMA), exponential smoothing (ETS), seasonal decomposition, and machine learning algorithms such as recurrent neural networks (RNNs) and long short-term memory (LSTM) networks.

84. Data science contributes to improving customer experience in retail by analyzing customer data, predicting purchasing behavior, personalizing marketing offers, and optimizing inventory management to meet customer demands and enhance satisfaction.

85. Data science plays a role in improving transportation systems and traffic management by analyzing traffic data, optimizing traffic flow, predicting congestion, and developing intelligent transportation systems to reduce travel time, minimize accidents, and improve overall transportation efficiency.

86. Data scientists handle bias and fairness issues in machine learning models by auditing models for bias, mitigating bias in training data, and implementing fairness-aware algorithms and techniques to ensure fair and equitable outcomes for all individuals or groups.

87. Structured data is data that is organized into a predefined format with a fixed schema, such as databases or spreadsheets, while unstructured data is data that does not have a predefined structure or format, such as text documents, images, or audio files.

88. Data science contributes to personalized recommendations in online platforms by analyzing user behavior, preferences, and interactions to generate personalized recommendations for products, services, or content, enhancing user engagement and satisfaction.

89. Common data preprocessing techniques used for text data in data science include tokenization, removing stop words, stemming or lemmatization, and vectorization methods such as TF-IDF (Term Frequency-Inverse Document Frequency) or word embeddings like Word2Vec or GloVe.

90. Data scientists handle data drift and concept drift in machine learning models by monitoring model performance over time, retraining models with updated data, and adapting models to changing data distributions or concepts to maintain model accuracy and relevance.

91. Data science contributes to optimizing pricing strategies and revenue management by analyzing customer behavior, market trends, and competitor pricing data to set optimal prices, segment customers, and maximize revenue and profitability.

92. Data scientists address the cold start problem in recommendation systems by using techniques such as content-based filtering, collaborative filtering, and hybrid approaches to provide recommendations based on user preferences, item attributes, or user-item interactions, even for new users or items with limited data.

93. Common techniques used for data imputation in data science include mean imputation, median imputation, mode imputation, regression imputation, and K-nearest neighbors (KNN) imputation, which fill in missing values in datasets to ensure completeness and accuracy for analysis.

94. Data science contributes to improving disaster response and emergency management by analyzing disaster data, predicting disaster risks, optimizing resource allocation, and developing early warning systems to mitigate the impact of disasters and save lives.

95. Data science plays a role in optimizing inventory forecasting and demand planning by analyzing historical sales data, market trends, and supply chain data to predict future demand, optimize inventory levels, and reduce stockouts and overstock situations.

96. Data scientists address bias and fairness issues in machine learning models by carefully selecting training data, auditing models for bias, and implementing fairness-aware algorithms and techniques to ensure equitable outcomes for all individuals or groups.

97. Structured data refers to data that is organized into a predefined format with a fixed schema, such as databases or spreadsheets, while unstructured data refers to data that does not have a predefined structure or format, such as text documents, images, or audio files.

98. Data science contributes to personalized recommendations in online platforms by analyzing user behavior, preferences, and interactions to generate personalized

recommendations for products, services, or content, enhancing user engagement and satisfaction.

99. Some emerging trends and future directions in the field of data science include the increasing use of artificial intelligence (AI) and machine learning (ML) techniques, the adoption of big data analytics and cloud computing platforms, the rise of edge computing and IoT (Internet of Things) technologies, the development of explainable AI and responsible AI practices, and the growing importance of data ethics, privacy, and security considerations.

100. How do data scientists address interpretability and transparency in complex machine learning models? - Data scientists address interpretability and transparency in complex machine learning models by using techniques such as model-agnostic interpretability methods, surrogate models, and explanation methods to explain model predictions and decision-making processes. These techniques help to provide insights into how the model makes predictions, identify important features and factors influencing the predictions, and improve trust and understanding of the model's behavior among stakeholders and end-users.

My Other Most Valuable Book For Students:

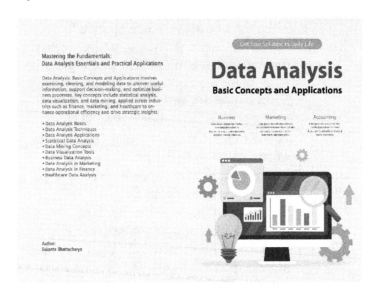

Purchase link:

https://www.amazon.com/dp/B0D4MB7WKW

Author: Sukanta Bhattacharya

www.ingramcontent.com/pod-product-compliance
Lightning Source LLC
La Vergne TN
LVHW051245050326
832903LV00028B/2587